THE INTERNAL COMMS PLAYBOOK

A Strategic Guide for Communications and HR Directors

Who Are Tired of Being Ignored

By Verster du Plessis

Published by Fish Star Media LTD

30 Smithbrook Kilns, Cranleigh, Surrey, GU6 8JJ, United Kingdom

Copyright © by Verster du Plessis

All rights reserved.

No part of this book may be reproduced in any form by electronic or mechanical means, including information storage and retrieval systems, without written permission from the author.

For Publishing/Editorial enquiries, please contact:
hello@fishstarmedia.com

For Adri, Christian, and Josh.

The only internal communications that actually matter.

Everything else is just practice.

CONTENTS

Introduction: Why Nobody Reads Your Emails (And What to Do About It)

PART ONE: THE CASE FOR A NEW APPROACH

    Chapter 1: The Perception Gap

    Chapter 2: The Internal Brand You Didn't Know You Had

PART TWO: THE STRATEGIC FRAMEWORK

    Chapter 3: Lead with Meaning, Not Information

    Chapter 4: Tell Stories Like You Mean It

    Chapter 5: The Waiting Game: Managing Uncertainty, Not Just Time

    Chapter 6: Friction, Ritual, and the Art of Intentional Design

    Chapter 7: Design Moments, Not Messages

PART THREE: THE PRACTICAL PLAYBOOK

    Chapter 8: Personalisation Without the Creepy

    Chapter 9: Support at the Point of Need

    Chapter 10: Pilots, Scarcity, and the Power of Social Proof

    Chapter 11: Showcasing the Craft

PART FOUR: MAKING IT WORK

Chapter 12: Measuring What Actually Matters

Chapter 13: The Operating System: Guardrails, Tiers, and Style Guides

Chapter 14: Getting Started: The First 90 Days

Conclusion: The Journey, Not Just the Train

Appendices

Appendix A: Templates and Checklists

Appendix B: Measurement Frameworks

Appendix C: Further Reading

Introduction

Why Nobody Reads Your Emails (And What to Do About It)

Here's an uncomfortable truth that every internal communications professional suspects but rarely says aloud: most of what you send goes unread, misunderstood, or forgotten within hours.

Not some of it. Most of it.

That CEO message you spent three weeks drafting? The one that went through legal, got softened by HR, then sharpened again because the CEO thought it "lacked punch"? About 40% of employees opened it. Of those, perhaps half read beyond the second paragraph. Of those, maybe a third could tell you what it actually said if you asked them the next day.

The all-staff announcement about the new operating model? It landed in inboxes at 9:47am on a Tuesday. Optimal send time, according to your analytics platform. It was buried under seventeen other emails by lunch. The people who did read it are now asking questions that were clearly answered in paragraph four. Which tells you everything you need to know about paragraph four.

The intranet page you lovingly crafted with FAQs, process diagrams, and a video from the project sponsor? It has 847 views. That sounds respectable until you remember you have 12,000 employees and this change affects all of them.

This isn't a failure of effort. Internal communications teams work extraordinarily hard. Harder than most of the organisation realises. You're producing content at a pace that would make a newsroom sweat, often with a fraction of the resources. You're navigating political minefields, translating executive-speak into human language, and somehow maintaining quality while everyone with a laptop considers themselves an editor.

The problem isn't effort. It's not even content, most of the time.

It's that we've been playing the wrong game entirely.

The Delivery Trap

For decades, internal communications has operated on what I call the "delivery model." The job, in this framing, is to get information from Point A (leadership's heads) to Point B (employees' heads) as efficiently as possible. Success is measured in reach, open rates, click-throughs. The goal is coverage. The metaphor is logistics.

And so we've optimised accordingly. We've built multi-channel strategies to catch people wherever they are. We've refined our send times based on engagement data. We've segmented our audiences and personalised our subject lines. We've made the trains run faster, more frequently, to more stations.

What we haven't done is ask whether anyone actually wants to be on the train.

Here's the thing about information: people don't value it by what it is. They value it by what it means. The same announcement, with identical words and identical facts, can feel exciting or threatening, significant or trivial, trustworthy or suspicious. It all depends on how it's framed, packaged, and delivered. Perception isn't a distortion of reality. Perception is the reality, at least when it comes to how people respond.

This isn't news to anyone in marketing. Brand teams have understood for decades that how something is presented matters as much as what it contains. They know that scarcity increases perceived value. That visible effort signals quality. That stories are remembered when facts are forgotten. That the "unboxing experience" shapes how people feel about the product inside the box. They know that some investments pay off immediately in sales, while others build brand equity that compounds over years. And they know you need both.

Internal communications, for reasons that probably seemed sensible at the time, has largely ignored these insights. We've treated employees as an audience to be reached rather than humans to be moved. We've measured delivery when we should have measured meaning. We've focused on the train when we should have focused on the journey.

The result is what you're living with now: an ever-increasing volume of communications competing for ever-decreasing attention, eroding trust with each ignored message, and a growing suspicion among leadership that "comms" is a cost centre rather than a strategic function.

It doesn't have to be this way.

Borrowing What Works

This book is built on a simple premise: the principles that actually work for internal communications aren't complicated. They're just borrowed from fields we rarely consult.

Behavioural economics has spent decades studying how people actually make decisions. Not the rational-actor fiction of classical economics, but the messy, biased, context-dependent reality. Those insights apply beautifully to how employees process organisational information.

Brand marketing has sophisticated frameworks for balancing short-term conversion with long-term trust-building. Those frameworks translate directly to how we should think about internal communications portfolios.

Experience design has cracked the code on making waiting feel shorter, making effort feel meaningful, and making moments memorable. All of that applies to how we package and deliver organisational news.

Even theme parks have something to teach us. Disney figured out decades ago that the queue is part of the ride. Managing the waiting experience is as important as the experience itself. Every change programme in your organisation is, in effect, a very long queue. We'll talk about how to design it.

What you'll find in these pages is a synthesis of these principles, translated into a practical framework for anyone responsible for internal communications. No jargon from academia. No case studies from companies so unlike yours that they're useless. Just a clear-eyed look at what actually works, why it works, and how to implement it without requiring a complete restructuring of your team or a 500% budget increase.

Some of what you'll read will feel intuitive. The kind of thing you suspected was true but couldn't quite articulate. Some of it will feel counterintuitive, even uncomfortable. That's intentional. If this book only confirmed what you already believed, it wouldn't be worth your time.

What's Ahead

Here's a preview of where we're headed.

Part One makes the case for a new approach. We'll examine why the current model fails. Not because internal communicators are incompetent, but because the model itself is optimised for the wrong outcomes. We'll introduce the concept of "brand" and "performance" communications, borrowed from marketing, and explain why the balance between them matters more than most organisations realise.

Part Two lays out the strategic framework. These are the principles that should anchor your approach: leading with meaning, telling better stories, managing uncertainty, designing rituals, creating moments rather than just messages. Each principle is grounded in research, but more importantly, each is practical. You'll finish each chapter with something you can actually use.

Part Three is the playbook. Specific tactics, templates, and techniques for putting the principles into practice. How to personalise without being creepy. How to run pilots that build belief. How to support people at the moment they need it, not just the moment you send. How to showcase the craft behind decisions in ways that build trust.

Part Four covers implementation. Measurement frameworks that track what actually matters. Operating structures that make good practice sustainable. And a 90-day roadmap for getting started when you can't change everything at once.

A Word on Tone

This book is direct, occasionally blunt, and not above the odd joke at the expense of corporate absurdity. That's intentional. Internal communications suffers from an excess of earnestness. We take ourselves terribly seriously, which makes it harder to see our own blind spots. A little irreverence is healthy.

But underneath the tone is genuine respect for the work. Internal communications, done well, is one of the most strategically important functions in any organisation. It's the connective tissue that turns strategy into action, leadership intent into frontline behaviour, corporate values into lived culture. When it works, it's invisible. Things just happen. When it fails, everything gets harder.

The people who do this work deserve better tools, better frameworks, and more strategic recognition than they typically receive. This book is an attempt to provide all three.

Three Ideas to Carry With You

The core mindset of this book can be summarised in three lines:

Don't just make the train faster. Make the journey feel better.

Psychological value is real value. Create it intentionally.

Sometimes the counterintuitive approach wins. Test it.

If those ideas resonate, keep reading. If they seem like soft thinking dressed up in business language, I'd gently suggest that's exactly the assumption that's been holding internal communications back for thirty years.

Let's get into it.

PART ONE

THE CASE FOR A NEW APPROACH

Chapter One: The Perception Gap

Why What You Send Isn't What They Receive

Picture the scene. It's 2pm on a Wednesday, and somewhere in your organisation, a senior leader has just approved the final version of an announcement that's been in development for six weeks.

The announcement concerns a restructuring of the operations function. Nothing dramatic. Some reporting lines are changing, a few teams are being consolidated, there's a new operating rhythm being introduced. Leadership sees it as a sensible efficiency play. The business case is solid. The changes are, in the grand scheme of things, fairly modest.

The communications team has done good work. The message is clear, the rationale is explained, the timeline is laid out, and there's a FAQ document covering the obvious questions. The tone strikes a reasonable balance between acknowledging that change is hard and projecting confidence that this is the right move. By any objective measure, it's a well-crafted piece of internal communication.

It lands in inboxes at 2:17pm.

By 2:19pm, three people in the Manchester office are in a huddle trying to decode what "consolidated support functions" actually means for their jobs. By 2:24pm, someone has posted in a WhatsApp group that "they're restructuring again, here we go." By 2:31pm, a manager in Birmingham is fielding panicked questions from her team, none of whom have actually read the FAQ. By 3pm, the narrative has fully escaped: this is the first phase of redundancies, leadership is cleaning house, and nobody's job is safe.

None of that was in the email. But it's what people received.

This is the perception gap. It's the central challenge of internal communications. What you send is not what people receive. The words on the screen are just the starting point. Raw material that employees process through layers of context, experience, anxiety, and interpretation before they arrive at meaning.

And here's the really uncomfortable part: the meaning they arrive at often has very little to do with your intentions.

The same announcement, with identical words and identical facts, can land as exciting or threatening depending on how it's framed. It can feel significant or trivial depending on how it's packaged. It can read as trustworthy or suspicious depending on what came before it. The gap between what you meant and what they understood isn't a bug in human cognition. It's a feature. And if you don't design for it, you're essentially hoping that 10,000 people will all independently arrive at the interpretation you intended.

Good luck with that.

The Information Illusion

Let's start with a foundational myth that internal communications needs to abandon: the idea that providing information creates understanding.

It seems logical. People don't know something, you tell them, now they know it. Communication complete. But this model, what academics call the "transmission model" of communication, is about as accurate as assuming that posting a letter guarantees the recipient will read it, understand it, agree with it, and act on it.

Information is not meaning. Information is the raw material from which meaning is constructed. And that construction happens inside each employee's head, using tools you don't control: their prior experiences, their current anxieties, their trust in leadership, their relationships with colleagues, their mental model of how the organisation works, and about a hundred other factors you probably haven't considered.

Here's a simple example. Imagine two employees receive the same message: "We're introducing a new performance management system starting Q2."

Employee A has been with the company for eight years. She's seen three previous "new systems" come and go, each announced with fanfare and abandoned within eighteen months. Her manager is supportive and gives her regular feedback regardless of what system is officially in place. Her interpretation: "Another initiative that won't last. I'll wait and see if it actually matters before I invest any energy."

Employee B joined six months ago. His previous employer used performance management punitively. Ratings were used to justify redundancies, and the annual review process was genuinely feared. He's still finding his feet and isn't sure where he stands. His interpretation: "They're building a case to manage people out. I need to be careful."

Same information. Completely different meanings. And neither interpretation was what you intended.

This is why the obsession with "clear communication" is necessary but not sufficient. Clarity helps. Muddled messages create even more room for misinterpretation. But clarity alone cannot close the perception gap. You can be crystal clear and still be completely misunderstood, because understanding isn't about the signal you send. It's about how that signal interacts with everything already in the receiver's head.

The Curse of Knowledge

In 1990, a Stanford psychology student named Elizabeth Newton conducted an experiment that should be required reading for every internal communicator.

She divided participants into two groups: "tappers" and "listeners." Tappers were given a list of well-known songs like "Happy Birthday" and "The Star-Spangled Banner" and asked to tap out the rhythm on a table. Listeners had to guess the song based on the tapping.

Before the listeners guessed, Newton asked the tappers to predict how often they'd be successful. Tappers predicted that listeners would guess correctly about 50% of the time.

The actual success rate? 2.5%.

The tappers were stunned. From their perspective, the song was obvious. They could hear the melody in their heads while they tapped. They couldn't understand how the listeners were failing to recognise something so clear.

This is the curse of knowledge. Once you know something, you cannot un-know it. And you systematically underestimate how hard it is for others to understand what seems obvious to you.

For internal communicators, this curse operates at multiple levels.

First, there's the subject matter itself. You've spent weeks immersed in the details of this restructuring, this system change, this policy update. You understand the rationale, the constraints, the trade-offs, the options that were considered and rejected. You know why paragraph three matters and why the timeline is what it is. Your audience has none of that context. They're encountering this information for the first time, probably while also thinking about the three other things they need to do before their 3pm meeting.

Second, there's the organisational context. You know that this announcement connects to the strategy discussion from the leadership offsite in March, which itself built on the customer feedback analysis from Q4. You know that "operational excellence" is one of the CEO's three priorities and that this initiative ladders up to it. Your audience may not even remember there was an offsite in March, let alone what was discussed.

Third, there's the emotional context. You've had time to process this change. You've asked questions, raised concerns, and arrived at a place of acceptance. Or at least resignation. You're sending the announcement from a position of relative equilibrium. Your audience is starting from scratch, experiencing in seconds the emotional journey that took you weeks.

The result is a persistent gap between what you think you've communicated and what people actually understood. You assume they got the main point; they fixated on a detail that worried them. You assume they read the whole thing; they skimmed the first paragraph and jumped to conclusions. You assume the context was clear; they had no idea why this was happening now.

Every time you think "but we explained that," remember the tappers. From your perspective, the melody is obvious. From theirs, it's just someone hitting a table.

Mental Accounting and the Inbox Hierarchy

Before your carefully crafted message even gets read, it faces a more fundamental challenge: getting noticed at all.

Behavioural economists use the term "mental accounting" to describe how people categorise and evaluate things based on subjective criteria rather than objective value. A £50 bottle of wine feels like a reasonable expense on holiday but an extravagance at home. A £20 fee feels acceptable when it's framed as "shipping" but outrageous when it's framed as "handling." Same money, different mental categories, different reactions.

Employees do the same thing with communications. Before they read a single word, they've already sorted your message into a mental category. And that category determines how much attention it receives, how charitably it's interpreted, and how likely it is to be remembered.

The primary sort happens based on sender. Messages from the CEO go in one bucket. Messages from HR go in another. Messages from IT go in a third. Each bucket carries assumptions. CEO messages are probably important but possibly just corporate theatre. HR messages are probably administrative and possibly about compliance training. IT messages are probably asking you to do something annoying.

These categories aren't fair, but they're real. And they're remarkably resistant to change. You can craft the most engaging, relevant IT communication ever written, and a significant portion of your audience will still approach it with the same enthusiasm they bring to cookie policy updates.

The secondary sort happens based on perceived relevance and effort required. Employees are constantly, unconsciously asking: "Is this for me? And what's it going to cost me to engage with it?" Messages that seem broadly generic get less attention than messages that seem specifically relevant. Messages that look long get less attention than messages that look short. Messages that seem to require action get sorted into "deal with later." Which often means "never."

This is why the subject line and opening paragraph matter so much. Not because of some email marketing trick, but because that's when the mental accounting happens. By the time someone has read your first sentence, they've already decided how much attention this message deserves. Everything after that either confirms or challenges that initial judgement.

The implication for communicators is significant. You're not just competing for attention with other messages. You're competing against the mental categories that employees have built up over years of experience with organisational communication. And most of those categories are not flattering.

What You're Actually Competing Against

Here's a question that internal communications teams rarely ask: what is actually competing for the attention we're trying to capture?

The obvious answer is "other emails" or "other communications." And that's partly true. There's certainly a volume problem. But it misses the real competition.

You're not competing against other work emails. You're competing against everything that's more interesting, more urgent, or more emotionally compelling than your message.

That includes the conversation happening in the team WhatsApp group about what last week's announcement "really" means. It includes the project deadline that's consuming 90% of someone's mental bandwidth. It includes the worry about a sick parent, the excitement about a weekend trip, the anxiety about whether that meeting went well. It includes the fact that Netflix exists and your intranet doesn't.

More fundamentally, you're competing against a baseline assumption that organisational communication is not worth paying attention to. This assumption has been built up over years. Decades, in some cases. Years of experience with corporate communications that were irrelevant, unclear, or simply boring. Every time an employee ignored an internal message and suffered no consequences, that assumption got a little stronger. Every time they did read a message and found nothing useful, it got stronger still.

This is the attention debt that internal communications has accumulated, and it compounds over time. Each ignored message makes the next one easier to ignore. Each disappointing experience lowers expectations further. You're not starting from neutral. You're starting from a deficit.

The good news is that this works in reverse, too. Consistently valuable, relevant communication can rebuild trust and attention over time. The bad news is that it takes longer to build than it took to destroy. And you don't get many chances to prove you've changed.

The Perception Gap in Practice

Let's make this concrete with an example of how perception gaps compound.

A company decides to relocate one of its offices. From leadership's perspective, this is a straightforward property decision. The current lease is expiring, the building doesn't meet modern requirements, and there's a better option available in a more accessible location. The move is positioned as an upgrade. Better facilities, easier commute for most people, investment in the working environment.

Here's what actually happens.

The announcement goes out. Before most people finish reading it, three things occur simultaneously.

First, someone realises the new location is further from a particular train station. This quickly becomes the dominant topic of discussion. Never mind that it's closer to two other stations. The one it's further from is the one people focus on.

Second, someone who's been through a previous office move shares their experience of the last one, which was poorly handled. This becomes the lens through which people view the current announcement.

Third, someone notices that the announcement doesn't mention what's happening to a particular team that was already rumoured to be under review. They conclude that this must be connected.

Within 24 hours, the internal narrative is: "They're making us move to a worse location, it's going to be chaos like last time, and this is probably the first step in cutting the team."

None of this was in the announcement. None of it was intended. But it's what people received.

The communications team, naturally, is frustrated. They were clear about the rationale. They included practical details. They offered Q&A sessions. And yet somehow, the message got away from them.

What they missed is that they were never just communicating about an office move. They were communicating into an existing context of experiences, anxieties, and assumptions. The announcement didn't exist in isolation. It was interpreted through everything that came before it.

So What Do We Do About It?

If the perception gap is inevitable, if you can never fully control how your messages are received, does that mean we should give up? Just send whatever and hope for the best?

Obviously not. But it does mean we need to shift our approach.

The first shift is from "information delivery" to "meaning creation." Instead of asking "What do we need to tell people?" we should ask "What do we need people to understand, believe, feel, and do?" Those are different questions with different answers.

The second shift is from assuming context to providing it. The curse of knowledge means we systematically underestimate how much framing people need. We should err on the side of more context, not less. Even when it feels redundant to us.

The third shift is from hoping for the best to designing for interpretation. If you know people will interpret your message through their existing anxieties, you can address those anxieties explicitly. If you know people will focus on the most worrying detail, you can get ahead of that. If you know people will compare this to a previous experience, you can acknowledge that comparison.

The fourth shift is from measuring delivery to measuring understanding. Opens and clicks tell you who received the message. They tell you nothing about whether the message landed as intended. We need better feedback loops.

The remainder of this book is about how to make these shifts in practice. But they all start from the same recognition: internal communication isn't about moving information from one place to another. It's about shaping how people make sense of their organisational world.

Get that right, and everything else gets easier.

Get it wrong, and it doesn't matter how clear your emails are.

Chapter Two: The Internal Brand You Didn't Know You Had

In 2012, two marketing researchers named Les Binet and Peter Field published a study that quietly revolutionised how the advertising industry thinks about effectiveness. They analysed hundreds of campaigns across decades of data and arrived at a conclusion that was both obvious and heretical: short-term sales activation and long-term brand building are different things, they work differently, and you need both.

This might sound unremarkable. Of course brand advertising and sales promotions are different. But the implications were profound. Binet and Field showed that the optimal balance between the two wasn't intuitive. Companies that focused too heavily on short-term activation (discount codes, limited offers, direct response campaigns) saw diminishing returns over time. Their marketing had to work harder and harder to achieve the same results. Meanwhile, companies that invested in long-term brand building created what the researchers called "pricing power" and "demand elasticity." Customers forgave mistakes, accepted price increases, and chose them over competitors even when the rational case was weaker.

The magic ratio, according to their research? Roughly 60% brand building, 40% sales activation. Not 50/50. Not 80/20. Approximately 60/40, weighted toward the thing that doesn't pay off immediately.

Now, here's what's interesting. Internal communications has its own version of brand and performance. We just don't talk about it that way. And because we don't, most organisations have the balance catastrophically wrong.

Let me explain what I mean.

Every piece of internal communication falls somewhere on a spectrum. At one end, you have what we might call "performance" communications. Messages designed to drive immediate action or deliver specific information. These are your how-to guides, your process updates, your deadline reminders, your "please complete this mandatory training by Friday" emails. They're functional. They have a clear purpose. Success is measurable: did people do the thing?

At the other end, you have "brand" communications. Messages that build understanding, trust, and connection over time. These are your vision statements, your values discussions, your "why we're doing this" explanations, your stories about customers and colleagues. They don't ask for immediate action. They don't have a click-through rate that matters. Their purpose is to shape how people think and feel about the organisation, its direction, and their place in it.

Most internal communications teams, if they're honest, spend about 90% of their energy on the performance end of the spectrum. And they can justify this easily: there's always something urgent, there's always a deadline, there's always a change that needs communicating, and leadership is always asking "but what do we need people to *do*?"

The result is what Binet and Field found in marketing: diminishing returns. Each communication has to work harder to cut through. Trust erodes. Cynicism builds. And when you really need people to pay attention, when there's a genuine crisis or a significant change, you've exhausted your credit.

You've been running your internal communications like a direct mail operation. And it's killing you.

The Trust Account

Think of your relationship with employees as a bank account. Every communication either deposits trust or withdraws it.

Performance communications are mostly withdrawals. Not because they're bad. They're necessary. But they're fundamentally asking something of people. Read this, do that, change your behaviour, complete this form, attend this session. Even when the request is reasonable, it costs attention and effort. It's a withdrawal.

Brand communications, done well, are deposits. They give people something: understanding, meaning, connection, reassurance. They answer the questions that performance communications assume away: Why does this matter? Where are we going? What's my role in all of this? Am I valued here?

An organisation that only makes withdrawals eventually overdraws the account. You've seen what this looks like. It's the company where every announcement is met with eye-rolls. Where employees assume the worst about leadership's motives. Where even good news is greeted with suspicion. Where change programmes fail not because they're poorly designed but because nobody believes in them anymore.

The trust account is empty. And at that point, no amount of clever messaging will fix it.

The opposite is also instructive. Organisations with healthy trust accounts can weather remarkable storms. They can announce difficult changes and have employees respond with concern rather than fury. They can make mistakes and be forgiven. They can ask for extraordinary effort and receive it. Not because their employees are naive, but because years of investment have built genuine belief in leadership's competence and intentions.

This is what Binet and Field called "pricing power" in the commercial context. In internal communications, we might call it "change elasticity." The organisation's capacity to absorb change without breaking. And like pricing power, it's not built through performance communications. It's built through sustained investment in meaning and trust.

The 60/40 Principle

So what's the right balance?

I'm going to suggest something close to Binet and Field's ratio: approximately 60% of your communication effort should go toward meaning, context, and trust-building. The remaining 40% handles the necessary performance stuff. The processes, deadlines, and calls to action.

I can already hear the objections.

"We don't have time for that. We're barely keeping up with the essential communications as it is."

"Leadership wants action, not philosophy. They'll never approve spending more time on 'why' when there's so much 'what' to cover."

"Our employees are drowning in information. They don't want more content about vision and values. They want us to get to the point."

These objections are understandable. They're also missing the point.

The 60/40 split isn't about creating more content. It's about rebalancing what you already create. It's about leading with meaning before mechanics. It's about investing thirty seconds at the start of an announcement to explain why this matters before diving into what's changing. It's about occasionally sending a message that doesn't ask for anything. A message that just tells a story, shares a success, or explains what's happening in the wider business.

And here's the counterintuitive bit: doing this actually makes your performance communications more effective, not less. When people understand the context, they're more likely to engage with the specifics. When they trust the source, they're more likely to read to the end. When they feel connected to the organisation's purpose, they're more likely to care about the process change you need them to adopt.

The objection that employees want you to "get to the point" is particularly worth examining. Yes, people are busy. Yes, they don't want waffle. But "getting to the point" doesn't mean stripping out meaning. It means making meaning clear and concise. The problem with most organisational communication isn't that it spends too much time on why. It's that it buries the why under jargon and hedging, if it includes it at all.

Employees don't want less meaning. They want more meaning, delivered efficiently.

What Brand Communications Actually Look Like

Let's get specific about what "brand" communications means in practice, because I'm aware this could sound fluffy.

Brand communications answer the questions that employees carry around but rarely ask aloud:

Where are we going? Not the strategic plan with its five pillars and seventeen initiatives, but the simple human story: what are we trying to become, and why does it matter?

Why should I care? What's in this for me, for my team, for the customers I serve? How does the organisation's success connect to my own?

Do the people running this place know what they're doing? Is there a coherent plan? Are we making progress? Can I trust that decisions are being made thoughtfully?

Am I valued here? Does leadership see employees as costs to be managed or people to be invested in? Do they understand what work is actually like on the ground?

What kind of place is this? What do we stand for? What would we never do? What can I be proud of?

Brand communications address these questions through a variety of formats: stories about customers and the impact of employees' work; honest explanations of strategic choices and their rationale; recognition of challenges and how they're being addressed; celebration of achievements that matter; acknowledgment of the human beings behind the job titles.

None of this requires elaborate production. Some of the most effective brand communications I've seen have been simple notes from leaders that took ten minutes to write. What they require is intention. A conscious choice to invest in meaning alongside mechanics.

Consider two versions of the same basic message:

Version A (Performance only): "Please complete your compliance training by March 15th. This is mandatory for all employees. Click here to access the training module."

Version B (Brand + Performance): "Last year, our compliance framework helped us identify and stop a fraud attempt that could have cost us £2.3 million and damaged relationships with three major clients. The training you're about to complete isn't box-ticking. It's the reason we caught that. Please complete it by March 15th. Link below."

Same action required. Same deadline. But Version B deposits something before it withdraws. It takes fifteen seconds longer to read and creates a completely different relationship with the request.

That's the 60/40 principle in miniature.

The Compounding Problem

Here's why getting this wrong is so dangerous: the effects compound in both directions.

Organisations that underinvest in brand communications don't just have a static problem. They have a worsening one. Each year of underinvestment makes the next year harder.

Trust erodes gradually, then suddenly. Employees don't wake up one day and decide to become cynical. They accumulate small disappointments: the announcement that didn't explain why, the change that seemed arbitrary, the leadership message that felt disconnected from reality, the recognition that never came. Each one is minor. Together, they create a pattern. And once the pattern is established, it becomes the lens through which everything else is viewed.

At that point, even good communication gets interpreted badly. Leadership announces an investment in employee development, and people assume there must be a catch. A manager shares positive feedback, and employees wonder what they're being softened up for. The organisation has trained its people to be suspicious, and now it's paying the price.

Meanwhile, organisations that invest in brand communications build a buffer that grows over time. Each positive experience reinforces the pattern. Trust compounds. Goodwill accumulates. When difficult news comes (and it always comes) there's a reservoir to draw on.

This is why the "we don't have time for this" objection gets it exactly backwards. You don't have time *not* to do this. Every month you spend in pure performance mode is a month of brand erosion. The longer you wait to address it, the deeper the hole you're digging.

The Organisational Forgiveness Factor

There's a specific benefit to brand investment that deserves its own discussion: organisational forgiveness.

Every organisation makes mistakes. Strategies don't work out. Systems fail. Leaders say the wrong thing. Decisions are made with incomplete information and turn out to be wrong. This is inevitable. The question is how employees respond when it happens.

In low-trust organisations, mistakes confirm the narrative. "See? They don't know what they're doing. They don't care about us. This is typical." The mistake becomes evidence for a pre-existing case against leadership. Recovery is slow and expensive.

In high-trust organisations, mistakes are contextualised. "That didn't work out, but I understand they were trying to do the right thing. I've seen them get it right before. I'll give them the benefit of the doubt while they fix it." The mistake is treated as an aberration, not a pattern.

This forgiveness factor is enormously valuable, and it's built almost entirely through brand communications. You cannot buy forgiveness in the moment you need it. You can only accumulate it in advance, through sustained investment in trust and meaning.

Think about the organisations that have weathered genuine crises. Product failures, public scandals, financial difficulties. The ones that emerged with their culture intact almost always had years of trust deposits to draw on. The employees who stayed and fought through the crisis did so because they believed in something larger than the immediate problem.

Now think about the organisations that collapsed under pressure that wasn't objectively worse. The difference was rarely the scale of the crisis. It was the trust account balance when the crisis hit.

Rebalancing Your Portfolio

If you accept the premise that most organisations have the brand/performance balance wrong, what do you actually do about it?

The first step is honest assessment. Look at your last month of communications and categorise each one: was it primarily asking for something (performance) or primarily giving something (brand)? Don't count brand elements that were perfunctory. A one-sentence nod to values before three paragraphs of instructions isn't balanced. Be rigorous. What's your actual ratio?

For most teams, this exercise is sobering. The number is usually somewhere between 80/20 and 95/5, weighted toward performance. That's the gap you need to close.

The second step is identifying low-cost brand opportunities. You don't need new channels or elaborate campaigns. You need to shift how you use what you already have. Every performance communication is an opportunity to lead with meaning. Every all-hands meeting is an opportunity to tell a story. Every leadership message is an opportunity to build trust.

The third step is protecting brand time. This is the hard part. Performance communications will always feel more urgent because they have deadlines attached. Brand communications feel optional because their payoff is diffuse and delayed. You have to consciously protect time for brand work, or it will always get squeezed out by the next urgent request.

Some teams I've worked with have found it helpful to set explicit ratios: for every four hours spent on performance communications, spend one hour on brand. Others build brand elements into their templates so they can't be forgotten. Others assign brand responsibilities to specific team members so someone is always advocating for it. The mechanism matters less than the commitment.

The fourth step is measuring differently. If you only measure performance metrics (opens, clicks, completion rates) you'll only optimise for performance. You need brand metrics too: trust scores, understanding measures, sentiment tracking. These are harder to capture and slower to move, but they're the indicators that actually predict organisational resilience.

The Long Game

I want to be honest about something: this chapter is asking you to invest in outcomes you won't see for months or years.

That's a hard sell. Internal communications teams are under constant pressure to demonstrate value, and value is usually defined in immediate terms. Did people open the email? Did they attend the session? Did they complete the training? These are the questions leadership asks, and they're the questions your metrics are set up to answer.

Asking for investment in brand communications is asking for faith in a different kind of return. One that shows up in employee resilience during change, in leadership credibility during crisis, in the accumulated trust that makes everything else easier.

I can't give you a spreadsheet that proves the ROI. What I can tell you is that every organisation I've seen that navigates change well has made this investment, whether they called it that or not. And every organisation I've seen that struggles with change, where every announcement is a battle, where cynicism is the default, where leadership has lost the room, has the same thing in common: years of underinvestment in meaning.

The balance won't fix itself. Every day you spend in reactive mode, answering the urgent requests and shipping the mandatory communications, is a day the deficit grows.

At some point, you have to decide to play the long game.

PART TWO

THE STRATEGIC FRAMEWORK

Chapter Three: Lead With Meaning, Not Information

There's a particular kind of meeting that happens in organisations everywhere, usually on a Monday morning. Someone from the project team presents an update on a major initiative. They share the timeline, the milestones achieved, the workstreams in progress, the risks being managed. Slides are shown. Acronyms are used. The presentation is thorough, professional, and completely forgettable.

At the end, someone asks: "So, what does this actually mean for us?"

The question hangs in the air. The presenter, who has just delivered fifteen minutes of information, looks slightly wounded. They answered that question, surely. It was all there in the slides.

But it wasn't. The slides contained facts. The question was about meaning. And those are not the same thing.

This is the central mistake of internal communications: we start with what's happening instead of what it means. We lead with information and hope meaning will follow. We bury the "so what" under the "what," and then wonder why nobody seems to care.

It's backwards. And fixing it is simpler than you think.

The Meaning Hierarchy

Human beings are meaning-making machines. We don't experience the world as raw data; we experience it as narrative, significance, implication. When something happens, our first question isn't "what are the facts?" It's "what does this mean for me?"

This is so fundamental to how we process information that we do it automatically, unconsciously, constantly. We can't help it. Give someone a piece of information and they will immediately, before they've even finished reading, start constructing meaning from it. They'll connect it to what they already know, assess what it implies, evaluate how it affects them.

The question for communicators is whether you're going to shape that meaning-making process or leave it to chance.

Most internal communications leave it to chance. They present information and assume people will arrive at the intended meaning on their own. This is a bit like giving someone a pile of ingredients and assuming they'll make the dish you had in mind. They might. They probably won't.

The alternative is to lead with meaning. To answer the "so what" before you explain the "what." To establish context before content, purpose before process, significance before specifics.

This isn't about dumbing things down or oversimplifying. It's about respecting how people actually process information and structuring your communications accordingly.

Think of it as a hierarchy:

First, meaning: Why does this matter? What's the significance? What problem are we solving or opportunity are we seizing?

Second, context: How does this connect to what we already know? Where does it fit in the bigger picture? What came before this and what comes next?

Third, information: What's actually happening? What are the specifics? What do people need to know?

Fourth, action: What do we need people to do? What's expected of them? What are the next steps?

Most communications start at level three and never really address levels one and two. The result is information that floats free, disconnected from meaning, competing for attention with everything else in people's inboxes.

Reverse the order. Start with meaning. Everything else follows.

The Framing Effect

In the 1980s, psychologists Daniel Kahneman and Amos Tversky demonstrated something that should have changed how we communicate forever: the way information is framed dramatically affects how people respond to it, even when the underlying facts are identical.

In one famous experiment, they presented people with a choice about a disease outbreak expected to kill 600 people. One group was told:

"If Programme A is adopted, 200 people will be saved. If Programme B is adopted, there's a one-third probability that 600 people will be saved and a two-thirds probability that no one will be saved."

Another group was told:

"If Programme A is adopted, 400 people will die. If Programme B is adopted, there's a one-third probability that nobody will die and a two-thirds probability that 600 people will die."

Same facts. Same outcomes. But the first framing emphasises lives saved, the second emphasises lives lost. In the first group, 72% chose Programme A. In the second group, only 22% did.

This isn't irrational, exactly. It's human. We respond to how things are presented, not just what they contain. Frame something as a gain and we become risk-averse; frame it as a loss and we become risk-seeking. Frame something as an opportunity and we lean in; frame it as a burden and we resist.

For internal communications, the implications are significant. The same organisational change can be framed in radically different ways:

"We're consolidating three regional offices into one central hub" versus "We're bringing our teams together into a state-of-the-art facility designed around how we actually work."

"We're implementing a new performance management system" versus "We're giving managers better tools to support your development and recognise your contributions."

"We're restructuring the department" versus "We're reorganising to put the right expertise closer to the decisions that matter."

Same facts in each case. Different meanings. Different emotional responses. Different levels of resistance.

This isn't spin. Spin is saying something untrue or deliberately misleading. Framing is choosing which true aspects of a situation to emphasise. Every communication involves framing choices, whether you make them consciously or not. The question is whether you're making those choices intentionally, in service of understanding, or leaving them to chance.

One useful test: how would you explain this change to a friend? Not a colleague, not a stakeholder, but someone you actually like and want to understand. You probably wouldn't lead with the process details. You'd start with why it matters, what problem it solves, why you think it's a good idea. That's the framing that should appear in your communications.

The "So What?" Test

Every piece of internal communication should be able to survive a simple but ruthless test: the "so what?" test.

Here's how it works. After every statement, ask "so what?" If the answer isn't obvious from the text itself, you haven't communicated meaning. You've only communicated information.

Let's try it:

"We are implementing a new customer relationship management system across all sales teams."

So what?

"The implementation will take place over Q2 and Q3, with training sessions scheduled for April."

So what?

"All sales data will be migrated to the new platform by June 30th."

So what?

If you're a salesperson reading this, none of your actual questions have been answered. Will this make my job easier or harder? Is my current process about to be disrupted? Will I lose access to my contacts during migration? Is this going to help me hit my targets or get in the way? What's wrong with the current system anyway?

Now let's try a version that leads with meaning:

"Our current CRM is costing us deals. Salespeople spend an average of eight hours a week on admin that should take two, and critical customer information is scattered across systems that don't talk to each other. We're fixing that."

So what?

"The new system consolidates everything into one place. Your contacts, your pipeline, your history with each customer, all accessible from a single screen. Early pilots showed a 60% reduction in admin time."

So what?

"We're rolling this out across Q2 and Q3, with proper training and support so you're not thrown in at the deep end. Migration happens in June, and we've built in a two-week overlap so you won't lose access to anything during the transition."

The second version answers the "so what?" at every stage. It leads with the problem being solved, shows what the change means for the reader, and provides practical details in service of that meaning.

The discipline of applying this test to every paragraph, every sentence really, transforms how you communicate. It forces you to think about meaning first and structure your communications around what people actually need to understand.

The One-Sentence Meaning

Here's an exercise I've found useful: before you write any significant communication, write one sentence that captures its meaning. Not what it's about. What it means. What's the significance for the reader?

This is harder than it sounds. The sentence can't be vague ("This is an important update about our strategy"). It can't be merely descriptive ("This explains the new procurement process"). It has to capture why someone should care.

Some examples:

For a reorganisation announcement: "We're putting customer expertise at the centre of every major decision, which means some teams are moving closer to the work that matters most."

For a benefits change: "We've traded a benefit most people didn't use for one that gives you more flexibility in how you work."

For a new system rollout: "We're eliminating the workarounds you've been doing for years and building the tool you actually need."

For a leadership change: "Sarah built the foundation; James is here to take us to the next level."

Once you have this sentence, it becomes the anchor for everything else. The opening paragraph should establish this meaning. The supporting details should reinforce it. The call to action should connect to it. If something in your draft doesn't serve this central meaning, it probably doesn't belong.

The sentence also becomes a useful test of whether you actually understand what you're communicating. If you can't articulate the meaning in one sentence, you probably don't have clarity on it yourself. That's worth knowing before you send.

The Story Spine

Meaning is best delivered through narrative. We covered this briefly in Chapter One, but it's worth going deeper here because story structure provides a natural framework for leading with meaning.

There's a simple structure, sometimes called the "story spine," that works for almost any organisational communication:

Origin: Where did this come from? What's the background? What situation gave rise to this?

Struggle: What problem or challenge are we addressing? What wasn't working? What opportunity were we missing?

Breakthrough: What's the solution? What have we figured out? What's changing?

Impact: What does this mean for people? What will be different? What's possible now that wasn't before?

This structure works because it mirrors how we naturally process meaning. We want to know where something came from before we evaluate where it's going. We want to understand the problem before we can appreciate the solution. We want to see the struggle before we can feel the significance of the breakthrough.

Let's apply this to a communication about a new hybrid working policy:

Origin: "For the past eighteen months, we've been learning what works about flexible working and what doesn't. We've surveyed every team, analysed productivity data, and tested different approaches in different offices."

Struggle: "What we found is that the current approach, informal arrangements that vary by manager, is creating inconsistency and frustration. Some teams feel pressured to be in the office more than they want; others feel disconnected because they're rarely together. Nobody's quite sure what's expected."

Breakthrough: "We're introducing a clear framework: three anchor days when teams are together, with flexibility around the other two. Every team will agree their anchor days by the end of the month, giving you both the collaboration time you need and the flexibility you've asked for."

Impact: "This means you can plan your week with confidence. You'll know when you need to be in, and you'll have genuine flexibility on the other days. Managers will have clear guidance instead of making it up as they go. And teams will have protected time together without requiring everyone to commute five days a week."

Notice how this structure naturally leads with meaning. The "what" doesn't appear until the breakthrough section, but by that point, the reader understands why it matters. The information is contextualised by the narrative that surrounds it.

Before and After

The best way to illustrate the power of leading with meaning is through direct comparison. Here are three typical internal communications and their meaning-led alternatives.

Example One: Technology Change

Before: "We are pleased to announce the implementation of ServiceNow as our new IT service management platform. ServiceNow will replace the current system effective April 1st. All employees will receive login credentials via email. Training materials are available on the intranet. For questions, contact the IT Service Desk."

After: "Submitting an IT request currently takes eleven clicks and an average of three days to resolve. That's not good enough.

We've invested in a new platform that cuts the process to three clicks and includes real-time tracking so you know exactly where your request stands. No more chasing, no more wondering if anyone's seen your ticket.

The new system goes live April 1st. Your login will arrive next week, and there's a two-minute video walkthrough if you want to see how it works. The IT Service Desk is standing by for questions, but honestly, this one should be pretty self-explanatory."

Example Two: Policy Update

Before: "The company has updated its expense policy effective March 1st. Key changes include: new approval thresholds, revised per diem rates for international travel, and updated documentation requirements. All employees must review the policy on the intranet and acknowledge understanding before submitting expenses. Non-compliant submissions will be returned."

After: "We've simplified the expense policy. The old one was 47 pages of legalese that nobody read and everyone worked around. The new one is 12 pages and written in English.

What's actually changing: higher thresholds before you need approval, better rates for international travel, and fewer receipts required for small purchases. We've also built clearer guidance into the expense system itself, so you shouldn't need to check the policy document every time.

Take five minutes to review the summary on the intranet. The new rules apply from March 1st."

Example Three: Organisational Change

Before: "Following a strategic review, we are restructuring the Operations division to better align with business priorities. Three regional teams will be consolidated into two, with enhanced centres of expertise supporting both. Affected employees will receive individual communications from HR. The transition will complete by end of Q2. An FAQ document is available on the intranet."

After: "For the past two years, our Operations teams have been stretched across a structure that made sense in 2019 but doesn't fit how we work now. Projects that should take weeks take months because expertise is scattered and decisions require too many handoffs.

We're fixing that. We're consolidating three regional teams into two, with dedicated specialists who support both. This means faster decisions, clearer ownership, and less time stuck in coordination meetings.

If your role is changing, you'll hear from your manager this week with specifics. For everyone else, the main impact is that things should start working better. We've put together an FAQ covering the most common questions. Link below."

In each case, the facts remain the same. What changes is the structure: meaning first, context second, information third, action fourth. The communications become longer, but they also become more effective. People actually understand what's happening and why it matters.

The Opening Paragraph

If there's one tactical takeaway from this chapter, it's this: rewrite your opening paragraphs.

The first paragraph of any communication is where meaning lives or dies. It's where people decide whether to keep reading or move on. It's where you either establish significance or lose them to the next email.

Most opening paragraphs fail this test. They start with announcements ("We are pleased to announce..."), procedures ("This message contains important information about..."), or background ("Following the Board meeting on March 15th..."). All of these delay meaning. They make the reader work to figure out why they should care.

A strong opening paragraph does three things: it establishes relevance (this matters to you), it creates clarity (here's what's happening), and it builds engagement (here's why it's interesting). Ideally, it does all three in two to three sentences.

Test your next communication by reading only the opening paragraph. Does it establish meaning? Does it answer the "so what?" If someone read only this paragraph and nothing else, would they understand the significance?

If not, rewrite it. Lead with meaning. Everything else follows.

Chapter Four: Tell Stories Like You Mean It

In 2009, a journalist named Rob Walker and a writer named Joshua Glenn conducted an experiment. They bought 100 cheap objects from thrift stores and garage sales. A ceramic horse, a wooden mallet, a plastic banana, that sort of thing. Average price paid: about $1.25 per item.

Then they asked 100 writers to create short fictional stories about each object. Not descriptions, not sales pitches. Stories. A narrative about the ceramic horse's journey from a grandmother's mantelpiece to a child's bedroom. A tale of the wooden mallet's role in a family's Sunday ritual.

They listed the objects on eBay, replacing the typical product description with the story.

The results were absurd. Objects purchased for $128.74 total sold for $3,612.51. A shot glass bought for a dollar sold for $76. A ceramic bust of a horse's head went from $0.99 to $62.95. The stories had added roughly 2,700% in perceived value.

This is not a chapter about selling trinkets on eBay. But if you're wondering why your carefully crafted communications aren't landing the way they should, the Significant Objects experiment holds part of the answer.

Stories do something that information cannot. They create value.

The PDF of Human Information

I've come to think of stories as the PDF of human information. The portable, universal format that people actually store and share.

Consider how information moves through an organisation. Leadership announces a strategy. That announcement contains facts, figures, rationales, timelines. It might even contain a clear explanation of what the strategy means. But what actually travels through the informal networks? What gets discussed in team meetings and mentioned over coffee?

Stories. Fragments of narrative. "Did you hear what happened in the Glasgow office?" "Apparently they tried this at headquarters and it was a disaster." "Sarah's team piloted it and she said it actually works."

These stories may or may not be accurate. They may or may not reflect what leadership intended to communicate. But they're what sticks. They're what spreads. They're what shapes how people actually think about what's happening.

This isn't a failure of human cognition, some irrationality to be corrected with better data. It's a feature. Our brains evolved to process narrative. Stories encode information in ways that align with how memory actually works: episodic, emotional, connected to characters and consequences. Facts presented outside of narrative are harder to remember, harder to share, and harder to act upon.

The practical implication is straightforward: if you want something remembered, make it a story. If you want something shared, make it a story. If you want something to change behaviour, make it a story about someone who changed their behaviour and what happened as a result.

You can fight this or you can use it. Fighting it doesn't work.

Why Stories Work

Let's get specific about what stories do that other forms of communication don't.

First, stories engage memory differently. When you hear a list of facts, your brain processes them in one area. When you hear a story, multiple regions light up. Not just language processing but also sensory cortex, motor cortex, emotional centres. This broader engagement creates stronger, more durable memories. You might not remember the three strategic priorities from last year's town hall, but you probably remember the story about the customer who called in tears because an employee went above and beyond.

Second, stories create emotional engagement. Neuroscience research has shown that when we hear stories, our brains release oxytocin, the same hormone associated with trust and social bonding. This isn't metaphorical; it's chemical. Stories literally create the conditions for people to care about what you're saying.

Third, stories enable simulation. When we hear about someone facing a challenge and making a decision, we mentally simulate being in their position. This simulation is practice. It prepares us to act similarly when we face similar situations. A story about a manager handling a difficult conversation well is, in a meaningful sense, training for managers who hear it.

Fourth, stories are inherently shareable. Facts require context to be transmitted accurately. Strip away the context and you get distortion. Stories carry their context with them. The setup establishes the situation; the narrative provides the meaning. Stories can travel from person to person and retain their significance in a way that data points cannot.

Fifth, stories create common ground. In any organisation, people have wildly different experiences of daily work. Stories provide reference points that everyone can share. "Remember when we were like that team in the story?" becomes a way of creating collective identity and shared understanding.

None of this means facts don't matter. Facts matter enormously. But facts are most powerful when they're embedded in narrative, when they serve as evidence within a story rather than standalone data points floating in space.

The Anatomy of an Organisational Story

Not every narrative is a story in the sense that matters for organisational communication. A chronological account of what happened isn't a story. A description of a process isn't a story. Even a case study with a beginning, middle, and end might not function as a story if it lacks the key ingredients.

What makes a story a story is structure. And the structure that works best for organisational purposes is simpler than most people think:

Setup: Establish a character in a situation. This doesn't have to be elaborate. A few sentences will do. "Three years ago, the Edinburgh team was in trouble. They'd missed targets for two consecutive quarters, morale was tanking, and their two best people were interviewing elsewhere."

Tension: Introduce a challenge, problem, or obstacle. This is where the story earns its power. Without tension, you don't have a story; you have a description. "They tried everything. New processes, revised targets, team-building events. But nothing seemed to shift the underlying problem. Then their manager, David, did something counterintuitive."

Insight: Show the realisation or decision that changed things. This is the hinge point, the moment that transforms the situation. "Instead of pushing harder, he started listening. He spent two weeks doing nothing but one-on-one conversations, really understanding what was blocking people. What he discovered surprised everyone."

Change: Demonstrate the outcome, what's different now. "Within six months, Edinburgh wasn't just hitting targets. They were leading the region. The insight David uncovered became a standard part of how we onboard new teams."

This structure works because it mirrors how we naturally make sense of change. We need to understand where things started before we can appreciate where they ended up. We need to feel the tension before we can value the resolution. We need to see the insight that drove the change, not just the change itself.

The structure also gives you a template. Whenever you need to communicate a change, an initiative, a new process, a strategic shift, you have a framework: what was the situation, what was the challenge, what did we figure out, and what's different now.

Finding Stories in Your Organisation

"That's all very well," I can hear you saying, "but where am I supposed to find these stories?"

Fair question. Most internal communications teams are so focused on pushing information out that they've never built the muscle for pulling stories in. But the stories are there. They're happening every day. You just need to know where to look.

Customer-facing teams are a goldmine. Sales, support, account management. These people hear stories constantly. The customer who almost left but stayed because of something an employee did. The deal that nearly fell through until someone found a creative solution. The support call that started with frustration and ended with gratitude. These stories are usually shared informally within teams and never make it to the wider organisation. Start asking for them.

Project teams at the end of major initiatives are another source. Every significant project has a narrative arc: the ambition, the obstacles, the breakthroughs, the lessons. Most project retrospectives focus on process improvements and miss the stories entirely. Add a question to your retrospectives: "What's the one story from this project that people should know?"

Long-tenured employees carry institutional memory. They know the stories that shaped the culture, the decisions that defined the organisation, the failures that taught lasting lessons. These stories are invaluable for onboarding and change management, but they exist only in people's heads until someone asks.

Leaders themselves have stories they may not realise are valuable. The decision that kept them up at night. The mentor who changed their perspective. The mistake they learned from. Leaders often think these personal stories are irrelevant to business communication, but they're exactly what makes leadership human and relatable.

The trick is making story collection systematic rather than accidental. Some organisations do this through formal programmes: story banks, narrative repositories, designated story collectors. Others simply add story prompts to existing processes: team meetings, performance conversations, project wrap-ups. The mechanism matters less than the habit.

The Story Bank

Speaking of systems, let me describe what a practical story bank looks like.

At its simplest, a story bank is a shared repository where stories are collected, categorised, and made accessible for communication purposes. It doesn't need to be elaborate. A well-organised shared document or simple database will do.

Each entry captures a few key elements: the story itself (ideally in the setup-tension-insight-change structure), the source (who told it, where it came from), relevant tags (theme, business area, use case), and permissions (can this be shared externally? Is it sensitive?).

Tags are particularly important because they enable retrieval. You might tag stories by theme (customer focus, innovation, resilience, collaboration), by business area (sales, operations, technology), by use case (onboarding, change management, leadership communication), and by format (suitable for all-hands, one-to-one, written communication).

When you need a story for a communication, and you should need stories regularly, you search the bank by relevant tags. Looking for something about adapting to change for a restructuring announcement? Check the resilience and change management tags. Need a customer story for the quarterly update? The customer focus tag should surface options.

The bank needs curation. Not every story collected will be worth using; some will be too specific, too complex, or simply not very good. Someone should review submissions and rate them for quality and versatility. Over time, you build a collection of tested, reliable stories that can be deployed when needed.

The bank also needs feeding. Make story submission easy. A simple form, a dedicated email address, a regular prompt in team communications. Recognise people who contribute good stories. Make it clear what you're looking for and why it matters.

The Customer Story Habit

If you implement one story-related practice, make it this: every all-hands meeting should include at least one story from outside the building.

Customer stories, or stories from whoever your organisation serves, have a unique power. They connect the abstract (strategy, metrics, targets) to the concrete (real people affected by the work). They remind employees why their work matters. They provide external validation that internal communications can't.

The story doesn't need to be extraordinary. In fact, ordinary stories often work better. The customer who had a smooth experience because systems worked as they should. The patient who received timely care because processes were followed. The client whose problem was solved by someone doing their job well. These stories validate the unglamorous daily work that makes organisations function.

The discipline of finding a customer story for every all-hands meeting forces you to maintain connection with the people you serve. It's easy, in the rhythm of internal operations, to become disconnected from external reality. The customer story habit keeps that reality present.

When you tell a customer story, ground it in specifics. Names (with permission), places, concrete details. "A customer in Leeds" is fine; "Margaret, who's been with us for twelve years and runs a small bakery in Headingley" is better. The specificity signals that this is a real person with a real experience, not a composite or a fabrication.

End the story with connection back to the room. What made Margaret's good experience possible? Whose work contributed to it? The point isn't just to feel good about a happy customer. It's to make visible the link between what people do and why it matters.

The 90-Second Origin Story

Every initiative, programme, or change should launch with a story. I call this the origin story, and it should take no more than ninety seconds to tell.

The origin story answers the question that's in everyone's mind but rarely asked aloud: "Where did this come from, and why should I care?"

Here's a template:

Thirty seconds on the situation that gave rise to this. Not comprehensive background, just enough context to understand why something needed to change. "Six months ago, we started hearing the same feedback from customers across every region. They loved our product but dreaded dealing with us when something went wrong."

Thirty seconds on what we learned or realised. The insight that led to the initiative. "When we dug in, we found the problem wasn't our people. It was our process. A customer with an issue had to navigate five different systems and talk to an average of three different people. No wonder they were frustrated."

Thirty seconds on what we're doing about it and why it should work. "This initiative creates a single point of contact. One person who owns the relationship from issue to resolution. It's based on a pilot we ran in the Midlands, where customer satisfaction jumped 34 points in three months."

Ninety seconds. That's all it takes. But those ninety seconds do something that a fifty-slide deck cannot: they create meaning and buy-in before you get to the details.

I'd encourage you to write these origin stories out and practice them. They're harder than they look. The temptation is always to add more context, more caveats, more background. Resist. The constraint of ninety seconds forces clarity.

Teaching Leaders to Tell Stories

Here's an uncomfortable truth: most leaders are bad at storytelling.

This isn't because they lack intelligence or communication skills. It's because they've been trained, by business schools, by corporate culture, by decades of experience, to value data, analysis, and abstraction over narrative and anecdote. Many leaders actively resist storytelling because it feels insufficiently rigorous.

If you're in internal communications, part of your job is helping leaders get over this resistance.

Start by reframing what storytelling is. For many leaders, "story" connotes fiction, embellishment, manipulation. Help them see that organisational storytelling is about illustrating truth, not inventing it. Stories are evidence. Specific, concrete evidence of principles in action. A story about a team that exemplified company values is data. It's just qualitative data, and it's more persuasive than most quantitative data.

Next, lower the bar for what counts as a story. Leaders often think they need something dramatic: a near-death business experience, a major crisis averted, a transformational breakthrough. These stories are rare. What's common and equally valuable: the small moment that revealed something important, the conversation that changed a perspective, the decision that turned out better than expected. Help leaders see that these ordinary moments are story-worthy.

Then, help them find their stories. This often requires guided conversation. Ask about moments of surprise, challenge, or change. Ask about people who influenced them. Ask about decisions that were difficult. Ask about times they changed their minds. The stories are there; they often just need to be surfaced and recognised.

Finally, coach them on delivery. The setup-tension-insight-change structure is a good starting point. But also: encourage specificity over abstraction, dialogue over summary, emotion over pure analysis. A leader who says "We faced a difficult quarter" is less compelling than one who says "I remember sitting in my office at 9pm, looking at the numbers, and thinking we might actually not make it."

Common Storytelling Mistakes

Let me save you some trial and error by describing the mistakes I see most often.

Mistaking chronology for narrative. "First we did this, then we did that, then we did the other thing" is not a story. It's a timeline. Stories need tension, a turning point, a transformation. If your account has no moment where something changed, it's not a story.

Leading with the lesson. Many organisational stories start with the moral: "This is a story about the importance of customer focus." This kills the narrative. You've told people what to think before you've given them reason to think it. Let the story create the meaning; don't impose the meaning before the story.

Making the organisation the hero. The best stories feature people, not entities. "The company achieved great success" is abstract and forgettable. "Sarah noticed something everyone else had missed, and what she did next changed everything" is concrete and engaging. Organisations don't make decisions; people do. Keep people at the centre.

Too much complexity. Organisational stories need to be simpler than the reality they represent. Multiple characters, subplots, tangents: these work in novels, not in all-hands presentations. One character, one challenge, one insight, one outcome. Anything more risks losing the audience.

Sanitising the struggle. Stories need real tension to work. If the challenge wasn't actually difficult, the resolution isn't meaningful. Don't pretend everything was easy. The struggle is what makes the story worth telling. "It was harder than we expected, and there were moments when we weren't sure we'd make it" is more compelling than a sanitised account where everything went smoothly.

Forgetting the "so what?" for the audience. Every story should connect back to why it matters to the people hearing it. The story about the Edinburgh team is interesting, but what makes it relevant? "That's why we're rolling out David's approach across all regional teams" or "That's the kind of initiative we want to see more of, and here's how we're supporting it." Don't leave the audience to draw their own connections.

The Story Test

Here's a simple test for whether your communication has sufficient narrative.

After you've drafted something, ask: can this be retold? If someone read this and wanted to share the key message with a colleague, could they? Is there something concrete enough to convey?

If the communication is pure information, dates, processes, requirements, it probably can't be retold. It has to be referenced, forwarded, looked up. It doesn't travel.

If the communication contains a story, a specific example, a narrative arc, a human element, it can be passed on. "Did you hear about the Edinburgh team?" "Let me tell you what happened with Margaret's bakery." Stories move.

This doesn't mean every communication needs a full story. Quick updates, process reminders, routine information: these can be purely functional. But any communication where you're trying to create understanding, build buy-in, or change behaviour should be able to pass the story test.

If it can't be retold, it won't be remembered. If it won't be remembered, it won't change anything.

Chapter Five: The Waiting Game

Managing Uncertainty, Not Just Time

In 2011, Uber had a problem. Customers were complaining about wait times. The company tried various approaches to reduce how long people actually waited. Optimising driver allocation, improving routing, expanding the fleet. All sensible stuff. All moderately effective.

Then someone had a different idea. Instead of reducing the wait, they changed how the wait felt.

They added the map.

You know the one. The little car icon moving through streets toward your location. The estimated arrival time counting down. The driver's name and photo. The ability to watch, in real time, as your ride approaches.

The map doesn't make the car arrive faster. It provides zero functional benefit whatsoever. And yet it transformed the waiting experience. Complaints dropped. Satisfaction rose. The same wait that felt interminable when you were standing on a kerb wondering if anyone was coming now felt manageable when you could see the car three streets away.

Uber had discovered something that internal communications desperately needs to understand: waiting isn't the problem. Uncertainty is.

The Psychology of Waiting

Researchers have been studying the psychology of waiting for decades, and their findings are remarkably consistent. The actual duration of a wait matters far less than how the wait is experienced. And the single biggest factor in how a wait is experienced is uncertainty.

An uncertain wait feels longer than a certain one. Significantly longer. Studies in healthcare settings have shown that patients who are told "you'll wait about thirty minutes" and then wait thirty minutes report higher satisfaction than patients who are told nothing and wait twenty minutes. The certain thirty-minute wait feels shorter than the uncertain twenty-minute one.

This makes no logical sense, but it makes perfect psychological sense. Uncertain waiting is cognitively expensive. Your brain keeps checking: How much longer? What's happening? Did they forget about me? Should I be worried? Is something wrong? This mental monitoring is exhausting. It also makes time feel like it's crawling.

Certain waiting, by contrast, allows your brain to relax. You know what's happening. You know when it will end. You can mentally allocate that time and move on to thinking about something else. The wait becomes a known quantity, and known quantities are easier to bear.

Now think about how most organisational change is communicated.

> *"We're restructuring the department. More details to follow."*

> *"The new system will be implemented in the coming months."*

> *"We're reviewing our options and will share an update when we have more to say."*

Every one of these statements creates uncertain waiting. Employees don't know what's happening, when it will happen, or what they should expect. Their brains go into monitoring mode. They start speculating, worrying, asking each other if anyone knows anything. The rumour mill spins up to fill the information vacuum.

And here's the thing: the organisation usually knows more than it's sharing. There's a timeline, even if it's provisional. There are milestones, even if they're subject to change. There are next steps, even if they're not finalised. But this information is held back, often with good intentions, to avoid creating false expectations. The result is an uncertainty tax that employees pay every day until the change is complete.

The Change Map

The Uber insight suggests a simple intervention: create visibility into the process.

I call this the change map. Like Uber's literal map, it shows people where things are and where they're going. It transforms "we're working on it" into something concrete and trackable.

A change map has a few essential elements.

First, milestones: what are the key stages of this change, and what does progress look like? Not every detail, but enough to understand the shape of the journey. "Phase 1: Design (January-February). Phase 2: Pilot (March). Phase 3: Rollout (April-May). Phase 4: Optimisation (June onwards)."

Second, current status: where are we right now? This needs to be updated regularly enough to be credible. A status indicator that hasn't changed in three weeks doesn't reduce uncertainty; it increases it. People start wondering if the project has stalled or if no one's bothering to update the status.

Third, what's next: what's the immediate next step, and when will it happen? This is the most important element. People can tolerate not knowing everything if they know something. "Next up: pilot team selection, announced by March 5th" gives people a concrete near-term event to anchor on.

Fourth, owners: who's responsible for this? Not in an accountability sense, but in a "who can I ask if I have questions" sense. Anonymous change is more threatening than change with a face attached.

The format doesn't matter much. It could be a dedicated intranet page, a regular update email, a physical board in the office, a Slack channel with pinned posts. What matters is that it exists, it's visible, and it's current.

Some organisations resist this because they're afraid of committing to timelines that might slip. This is understandable but counterproductive. People can handle "we expected to finish the pilot by March 15th, but we've hit some issues and it's now looking like March 30th." What they can't handle is silence. Silence gets interpreted as secrecy, incompetence, or bad news being hidden.

Be visible about uncertainty when it exists. "We're not yet sure whether we'll need to extend the pilot; we'll know by March 10th" is better than saying nothing. You're being honest about what you don't know, and you're giving people a date when they'll know more.

The "You're Here" Module

Here's a specific technique that works remarkably well: add a "You're here. Next up..." module to any communication about an ongoing programme.

It's exactly what it sounds like. A visual or textual indicator that shows where in the process things currently stand and what the immediate next step is.

For a system implementation, this might look like:

"You're here: Training phase (week 3 of 6). Next up: Practice environment access (March 12th)."

For a reorganisation:

"You're here: Team assignments confirmed. Next up: New structure goes live (April 1st). First new-team meeting (April 3rd)."

For a policy change:

"You're here: Consultation period. Next up: Final policy published (February 28th). New policy effective (March 15th)."

This module should appear in every communication related to the programme. Every email, every update, every FAQ document. It becomes a consistent orientation device that helps people locate themselves in the change journey.

The psychological effect is significant. Instead of "this change is happening to me and I don't know what's going on," the feeling becomes "I'm at this point in a process, and I know what comes next." That's a fundamentally different experience of change.

Predictable Cadences

The other element of reducing uncertainty is predictability. Not just in what you communicate, but in when you communicate.

Think about how anxiety-inducing it is to wait for news that might come at any moment. You keep checking your email. Every time your phone buzzes, you wonder if this is it. You can't fully focus on anything else because part of your brain is always monitoring for the update.

Now think about how different it feels when you know the update will come on Wednesday at 2pm. You might still be anxious about the content, but you're not anxious about the timing. You can stop monitoring. You know when you'll know.

Predictable communication cadences create this effect at organisational scale.

Some organisations do this well. "Strategy updates happen on the first Monday of each month." "Project status is shared every Friday afternoon." "The CEO sends a note every Wednesday." These rhythms reduce uncertainty even when the content is uncertain. People know when to expect information, so they're not constantly wondering if they've missed something.

I sometimes call this the Tuesday/Thursday rule, though the specific days don't matter. The principle is: establish a regular rhythm for updates on any significant change, and stick to it religiously.

During a major restructuring, this might mean: "Every Tuesday, we'll share what's been decided. Every Thursday, we'll host office hours for questions." During a system implementation: "Status updates every Friday; training sessions every Monday and Wednesday."

The cadence should match the pace of the change and the level of employee concern. A three-year digital transformation might need monthly updates. A restructuring that affects people's jobs needs weekly, maybe even more frequent, communication.

Whatever cadence you choose, the key is consistency. If you say Tuesday, it has to be Tuesday. If you miss a week, you've undermined the entire point. People's trust in the predictability takes weeks to build and one missed update to destroy.

Reframing Waiting as Preparation

There's a second strategy for managing the waiting experience, and it works in a completely different way. Instead of making the wait feel shorter through visibility, you make the wait feel purposeful through activity.

The psychological principle here is simple: time that's being used feels different from time that's being wasted. Waiting while doing nothing is tedious. Waiting while preparing is productive.

Consider two employees waiting for a new system to launch. Employee A has been told the launch is in six weeks and to wait for further instructions. Employee B has been told the launch is in six weeks, and here's what they'll be doing in the meantime: week one is orientation materials; week two is practice exercises; week three is their first session with the new workflow; and so on.

Same six weeks. Completely different experience. Employee A is in limbo. Employee B is on a journey.

This is the principle of reframing waiting as preparation. Instead of a gap to be endured, the pre-change period becomes an equipping phase. Time doesn't just pass; it gets filled with purposeful activity that builds readiness for what's coming.

The activities don't need to be onerous. They can be small: review these materials, attend this briefing, complete this exercise, meet your new team, set up your new account. The point isn't to create busywork. The point is to give people something meaningful to do with their anticipation.

This approach also has a practical benefit beyond psychology. People who spend six weeks preparing for a change are actually more ready for it than people who spend six weeks waiting. The preparation isn't just a perception management trick; it's genuinely useful. But even if the preparation had zero practical value, it would still be worth doing for the psychological benefit alone.

The Pre-Launch Window

Most change programmes treat the period before go-live as a countdown. "Four weeks until launch. Three weeks. Two weeks. One week. Go." The countdown creates anticipation, but it doesn't create readiness.

A better approach is to design the pre-launch window as a structured preparation phase with its own milestones and deliverables.

Let's say you're implementing a new procurement system that goes live on May 1st. Here's what a structured pre-launch might look like:

Six weeks out (mid-March): Orientation. Everyone who'll use the system receives an overview. Not training, just context. What is this system, why are we implementing it, what will be different. At the end of this week, milestone: everyone has acknowledged they understand what's coming.

Four weeks out (early April): Exploration. Practice environment opens. Users can poke around, see the interface, understand the basic flow. No pressure to master anything; just familiarisation. Milestone: everyone has logged in at least once.

Three weeks out (mid-April): Training. Structured sessions on key workflows. This is where the real learning happens. Milestone: everyone has completed core training and passed the basic competency check.

Two weeks out (late April): Practice. Users run through realistic scenarios in the practice environment. Questions are collected and addressed. Milestone: everyone has completed at least three practice transactions.

One week out: Final prep. Accounts are set up, bookmarks are saved, cheat sheets are distributed, support channels are confirmed. Milestone: everyone is ready to go on day one.

Notice how this transforms the pre-launch experience. Instead of six weeks of waiting, it's six weeks of progressive engagement. Each week has a purpose. Each milestone provides a sense of progress. By the time launch day arrives, users aren't anxious about the unknown; they've already been working with the system for weeks.

Building in Buffers

One more practical consideration: build buffer time into your change timelines, and be transparent about it.

Most projects run late. This is so universal that we should probably stop being surprised by it. When you communicate a timeline with no buffer, you're setting yourself up for a credibility problem. The first delay, and there will be one, damages trust. Subsequent delays compound the damage.

A better approach is to build realistic buffers into your communicated timeline and to be honest about them. "We're planning to go live in early May. We've built in two weeks of contingency, so the latest would be mid-May. We'll confirm the exact date by April 15th."

This doesn't feel like hedging; it feels like competence. You're showing that you understand how projects actually work. You're being honest about uncertainty rather than pretending it doesn't exist. And you're giving yourself room to deliver on time rather than setting up a pattern of missed deadlines.

When you do deliver early, or even on time given how low expectations often are, you get a credibility boost. "They said early May, contingency to mid-May, and they launched on May 3rd. These people know what they're doing."

When You Don't Have Answers

Sometimes uncertainty is genuine. You don't know the timeline because it depends on decisions that haven't been made. You don't know the impact on specific teams because the details are still being worked out. You can't provide visibility because there's nothing to see yet.

This is uncomfortable, and the temptation is to say nothing until you have something definitive. Resist this temptation.

Employees know that change is complicated and that plans evolve. What they can't tolerate is the feeling that they're being kept in the dark or forgotten. Even when you don't have answers, you can provide communication that reduces uncertainty.

Acknowledge the uncertainty explicitly: "We know you have questions about how this will affect your team. We don't have those answers yet. The design work is still in progress. Here's what we do know..."

Explain what's driving the uncertainty: "The timeline depends on the technology assessment, which is happening now. We'll know more when that's complete, expected mid-March."

Commit to a next update: "We'll send another update by March 20th, even if we don't have final answers. We'll share what we know at that point and what's still being worked out."

Create a channel for questions: "We've set up a dedicated space for questions about this change. We can't answer everything yet, but we're tracking what people want to know and will address these as soon as we can."

This approach is radically different from silence, even though it doesn't provide much concrete information. It shows that the organisation is aware of employees' uncertainty and is actively working to address it. That alone reduces anxiety.

The Uncertainty Audit

Here's a practical exercise. Take any major change or initiative currently underway in your organisation and answer these questions:

Can employees see where the initiative currently stands? Is there a visible status indicator that's regularly updated?

Do employees know what happens next? Is there a clear next milestone, and do they know when it will occur?

Is there a predictable communication cadence? Do people know when they'll receive updates?

Is the waiting period structured with preparatory activities? Or are people just waiting?

Can employees get answers to their questions? Is there an obvious, accessible way to ask questions and receive responses?

If the answer to any of these is "no," you have an uncertainty problem. And that uncertainty problem is costing you. In anxiety, in rumour, in trust, in the cognitive load people carry while waiting for news.

The good news is that these problems are fixable without requiring new information. You probably already have the timelines, status updates, and next steps. They're just not being communicated in a way that creates visibility. The change map, the "You're here" module, the predictable cadence: these are communication choices, not information creation. They take effort to implement, but they don't require waiting for decisions to be made.

The Uber map didn't make the car come faster. It just made the wait bearable. Your change map can do the same thing.

Chapter Six: Friction, Ritual, And The Art Of Intentional Design

In the 1950s, an American food company launched a revolutionary product: instant cake mix. Just add water, stir, and bake. It was faster, easier, and more convenient than traditional baking. It should have been a massive success.

It flopped.

The company was baffled. They'd removed all the effort from baking. Why weren't customers delighted?

They hired psychologists to investigate. What they discovered was counterintuitive: the product was too easy. Housewives, the target market at the time, felt that simply adding water wasn't really baking. There was no sense of accomplishment, no feeling of having contributed something meaningful. The convenience had stripped out the satisfaction.

The solution was elegant. They changed the recipe to require adding an egg. Just an egg. The actual difference in effort was trivial. But psychologically, it transformed everything. Now you were baking. You were contributing an ingredient. The cake was, in some meaningful sense, yours.

Sales took off.

This story has become famous in product design circles as the "just add an egg" principle. And it contains a profound insight for internal communications: sometimes friction is the feature, not the bug.

The Friction Paradox

Most organisations have a contradictory relationship with friction. On one hand, they're filled with unnecessary obstacles that make work harder than it needs to be. Finding the right contact takes fifteen minutes. Getting approval requires four signatures. Accessing basic information means navigating three systems and remembering two passwords.

On the other hand, these same organisations often strip friction from places where it would actually help. Initiatives launch without ceremony. Milestones pass without acknowledgment. Major decisions are announced via email and never spoken of again.

The result is the worst of both worlds: friction where it frustrates, absence of friction where it would create meaning.

Getting this right requires understanding what friction actually does. Friction slows things down. That's usually bad. Nobody wants unnecessary delays. But slowing down also creates space for attention, reflection, and significance. A moment of friction says: this matters enough to pause for.

The art is in knowing which friction to remove and which to preserve or even add. Remove the friction that creates frustration without value. Add friction that creates meaning, ownership, or memory. The goal isn't frictionless. It's intentionally frictioned.

Invisible Friction

Let's start with the friction that needs to go: the invisible blockers that slow people down without anyone quite realising it.

Invisible friction is called that because it's often unnoticed by the people who design systems and communications. They know how things work, so the obstacles aren't obstacles for them. But for employees encountering something for the first time, these small barriers compound into significant resistance.

Consider something as simple as finding out who to contact about a question. In many organisations, this is genuinely difficult. The org chart is out of date. The intranet search returns seventeen results, none obviously right. The person who used to handle this has moved on, and nobody updated the documentation. Eventually, you ask a colleague who asks another colleague who thinks they might know someone.

This is friction. It's not deliberate. Nobody designed the system to be confusing. But it's real. And it has costs: time wasted, questions unanswered, problems unresolved, and a gradual learned helplessness where people stop trying to find information because it's too hard.

Or consider the structure of communications themselves. An announcement that buries the action item in paragraph four. A policy document that requires reading 3,000 words to find the one sentence that actually matters to you. An email that says "see attached" when the attachment is a 47-slide deck with no executive summary. Each of these creates friction. Small barriers that reduce the likelihood of comprehension and action.

The tricky thing about invisible friction is that it's genuinely invisible to insiders. You've learned the workarounds. You know which slide has the important information. You remember that "consolidated support services" actually means the IT help desk. The friction has become so familiar that you've stopped seeing it.

This is why friction audits need fresh eyes. New employees are your best source of insight here. They haven't yet learned to navigate the obstacles, so they still feel them. Exit interviews are another goldmine: people leaving often have accumulated frustrations they're finally willing to articulate.

The Friction Audit

Here's a practical framework for identifying unnecessary friction in your communications.

Start with the employee journey for any significant communication or change. Map out every step from "becomes aware" to "successfully acts." For a new policy, this might be: receives announcement, understands relevance, finds full policy, locates relevant section, understands requirements, identifies how to comply, takes action, confirms completion.

At each step, ask: what could go wrong? What might stop someone from progressing? What questions might they have that aren't answered? What assumptions are we making about their knowledge or capability?

Then, actually test it. Find someone unfamiliar with the communication and watch them try to act on it. Don't help. Don't explain. Just observe. You'll be amazed at where people get stuck. The link that's obvious to you but invisible to them. The jargon that you've forgotten is jargon. The step that seems self-evident but isn't.

Common friction points to look for:

Buried information. The key message or action is hidden in a longer communication. People have to work to find what matters.

Missing context. The communication assumes knowledge that readers don't have. Acronyms, references to previous communications, assumed familiarity with processes or people.

Unclear ownership. It's not obvious who to contact with questions, or the contact information is hard to find, or the listed contact is wrong.

Broken pathways. Links don't work, documents have moved, referenced resources no longer exist.

Excessive steps. Completing the required action requires more clicks, approvals, or handoffs than necessary.

Format friction. The communication is in a format that's hard to access. A video when people want text, a dense document when people want a summary, a mobile-unfriendly design when people are on their phones.

For each friction point you identify, ask: is this necessary? Does it serve a purpose? If not, remove it. If it does serve a purpose, make sure the purpose is worth the cost.

Intentional Ritual

Now for the other side of the equation: friction that should be added, not removed.

Rituals are intentional friction. They're moments that slow things down, require participation, and mark significance. And they're almost entirely absent from most organisational communication.

Think about how major initiatives typically launch. An email goes out. Maybe there's a town hall where it's mentioned among six other agenda items. A page appears on the intranet. And that's it. The thing is launched. On to the next thing.

Now think about how that same launch might feel with intentional ritual. A dedicated session, not a mention in a broader meeting, but its own moment. An opening that acknowledges the work that led to this point. A human story about why this matters. A visual artifact, something tangible that marks the occasion. A moment of participation, a question to respond to, a commitment to make, a small act that involves the audience. A clear close that marks the beginning of what comes next.

Same information conveyed. Completely different experience. The ritual version takes more time. It requires more effort. It creates friction. And that friction is precisely what makes it memorable and meaningful.

Rituals work because they signal significance. When an organisation takes time to mark a moment, when it slows down and creates ceremony around something, it's communicating that this matters. The friction is the message.

This is why cultures throughout human history have created rituals around important transitions: births, deaths, marriages, coming-of-age, harvest, new year. The ritual doesn't change the underlying reality, but it changes how we experience and remember it. Organisations need rituals for the same reasons.

Five Rituals You Can Implement Now

Let me be specific about what organisational rituals look like in practice. Here are five that any team can implement without requiring approval, budget, or elaborate planning.

The origin story opening. Every time you launch an initiative, programme, or significant change, open with ninety seconds of narrative. Where did this come from? What problem are we solving? Who worked on this and why do they care? This ritual takes almost no time but transforms a transactional announcement into a human story. We covered the structure in Chapter Four; the ritual is committing to doing it every time.

The customer story moment. Every all-hands, team meeting, or significant gathering includes at least one story from the people you serve. Not metrics about customers, a story about a specific customer. This ritual keeps external reality present in internal conversations and reminds people why their work matters. Make it a non-negotiable agenda item, not something that gets cut when time runs short.

The milestone marker. When a project hits a significant milestone, mark it. This doesn't require a party or elaborate celebration, though those are fine too. It can be as simple as a dedicated message that says: "We said we'd reach this point by this date. We did. Here's who made it happen and what it means." The ritual is the pause to acknowledge progress before rushing on to the next thing.

The "just add an egg" invitation. Before finalising something significant, a new policy, a set of values, a programme design, invite input. Not comprehensive consultation, which has its place but is a different thing. Just a small moment of co-creation: "We've drafted the three principles. Before we finalise, what's missing? What would you add?" The input you receive may or may not change anything. The ritual of invitation creates ownership regardless.

The closure ceremony. This might be the most neglected ritual in organisational life. Projects end, initiatives conclude, programmes wrap up, and nothing marks the ending. People move on to the next thing without any acknowledgment of what was accomplished. A closure ceremony doesn't need to be elaborate: a brief retrospective, a summary of what was achieved, acknowledgment of contributors, lessons to carry forward. The ritual says: this mattered, it's complete, and we're intentionally closing this chapter.

The "Just Add an Egg" Principle

Let's go deeper on the fourth ritual, because it connects to something important about human psychology and ownership.

The cake mix story illustrates a broader principle: people value what they contribute to. Effort creates attachment. When you put something of yourself into a project, a decision, a document, even something small, it becomes partly yours.

Internal communications typically miss this opportunity entirely. Decisions are made, policies are written, initiatives are designed, and then they're announced to employees as finished products. Here's the new thing. It's done. Comply.

This approach maximises efficiency and minimises ownership. People receive the output but weren't part of the process. They have no stake in the result. Why would they feel invested in something they had no hand in creating?

The "just add an egg" principle suggests a different approach: build in small moments of contribution that create ownership without slowing things down significantly.

Before finalising the new values statement, share a draft and ask: "What's the one word or phrase that feels most true to your experience here?" You might get useful input. More importantly, everyone who responds now has a stake in the outcome.

Before launching the new recognition programme, invite people to nominate the first recipients. The programme becomes theirs in a way it wouldn't if you simply announced the winners.

Before rolling out the updated expense policy, ask teams to identify which of the old policy's pain points they most want addressed. When the new policy addresses those points, it's a response to their input, not an imposition from above.

The key is that the contribution needs to be real but not onerous. A five-minute input, not a two-week consultation process. A genuine question, not a fake one where the decision has already been made. The egg needs to be easy to add, but it needs to actually go into the cake.

Designing Moments

Let's zoom out and talk about what all of this adds up to: the practice of designing moments, not just messages.

A message is information transferred. A moment is an experience created. The difference is intention and craft.

Consider a typical organisational announcement: new leadership appointment. The message version: "We are pleased to announce that Sarah Chen has been appointed as Chief Operating Officer, effective March 1st. Sarah joins us from [previous company] where she served as [previous role]. Please join us in welcoming Sarah to the team."

This conveys the information. It's fine. It's also completely forgettable. It creates no particular feeling, no sense of significance, no memory.

The moment version might include: a short video of Sarah talking about why she's excited to join and what she hopes to accomplish. A story about what attracted her to the organisation. A message from the CEO explaining why Sarah was chosen and what her appointment signals about the company's direction. A visual element, a professional photo, yes, but perhaps also something that shows Sarah as a person, not just an executive. An invitation to an informal meet-and-greet. A way for people to send welcome messages.

Same information. But now it's an experience. There's texture, humanity, significance. People will remember this appointment because there was something to remember.

Not every communication needs to be a designed moment. Routine updates, process information, administrative notices, these can and should be efficient. But significant communications, leadership changes, strategic shifts, major initiatives, organisational milestones, deserve the investment of intentional design.

The question to ask is: how do we want people to feel after receiving this? If the answer is "informed," a message will do. If the answer includes feelings like "inspired," "valued," "connected," or "proud," you need to design a moment.

The Premium Template

For your most important communications, what I'd call Tier 1 announcements, it's worth developing a premium template that you use consistently.

The template should include several elements:

A human opening. Not "We are pleased to announce" but something that establishes meaning and connection. A story, a statement of significance, a personal note from a leader.

A clear narrative. The setup-tension-insight-change structure from Chapter Four works well here. What's the context, what's the challenge or opportunity, what have we figured out, what's changing as a result.

Visual craft. This doesn't mean expensive production. It means thoughtful presentation. A considered layout. Quality imagery. Consistent branding. Attention to detail that signals care.

A tangible artifact. Something people can keep, share, or display. This might be a one-page summary, a poster, a digital badge, a reference card. The artifact extends the moment beyond the initial communication.

A human close. A named person taking ownership. An invitation to respond or connect. Something that leaves people with a sense of who's behind this, not just what's being announced.

The premium template takes more effort than a standard email. That's the point. The effort is visible. It signals that this communication matters more than routine updates. The friction of production becomes part of the message.

Protecting the Magic

There's a balance to strike here, and I want to name it explicitly: you can show craft without showing everything.

Some organisations, in their enthusiasm for transparency, share too much of the process. Every draft, every debate, every version of the decision. The intention is good. People want to show their working. But the effect can be to undermine the final product. If you've seen seventeen iterations, the final version feels arbitrary rather than definitive.

Think about how great experiences work. A magic show doesn't explain every trick. A restaurant doesn't walk you through the kitchen chaos. A film doesn't include a documentary about its own production. These experiences work partly because they maintain some mystery. You see the craft but not the full machinery.

Organisational communication can learn from this. Share enough process to build trust. Let people see that thought went into decisions. But don't turn every announcement into a documentary about its own creation. Preserve some "magic," some sense that the thing you're receiving is the result of care and consideration, not just the latest draft that happened to stick.

The principle is: earn trust through visible craft, create impact through selective reveal. Show the artisan, not the entire workshop.

The Ritual Audit

As a counterpart to the friction audit, here's a ritual audit for your organisation.

Map the significant moments in your organisational calendar. Strategy launches, reorganisations, major system changes, leadership transitions, annual milestones, project completions.

For each moment, ask: what ritual currently exists? Is there any intentional marking of this occasion, or does it just happen?

For moments with no ritual: what's lost? What would be different if this moment were marked with intention? What feeling or memory are you failing to create?

For moments with existing rituals: are they working? Do they feel meaningful or perfunctory? Are they creating the significance they should, or have they become empty gestures?

Identify the gaps. Where are significant moments passing unmarked? Where are existing rituals falling flat?

Design interventions. For one or two high-impact moments, create or redesign the ritual. Keep it simple. Ninety seconds of intention is better than elaborate ceremony that nobody has time for.

The goal isn't to ritualise everything. That would be exhausting and would dilute the impact. The goal is to identify the moments that genuinely matter and ensure they receive the intentional friction they deserve.

The Both-And

I want to close this chapter by emphasising that friction reduction and ritual creation aren't competing priorities. They're complementary.

The organisations that get this right are ruthless about removing unnecessary friction, the barriers that slow people down and create frustration without value, and equally intentional about adding meaningful friction where it creates significance.

They make it easy to find information, contact the right person, complete routine tasks, and navigate daily operations. And they make it special to launch a major initiative, mark a milestone, welcome a new leader, or close a chapter.

The worst organisations have this backwards. They're filled with obstacles that serve no purpose and devoid of rituals that create meaning. Work is hard in all the wrong ways and easy in all the wrong ways.

The instant cake mix failed because it removed the wrong friction. The solution wasn't to make baking harder across the board. It was to identify the one moment of contribution that made the difference between "just add water" and "I made this."

Your internal communications face the same challenge. Find the friction that's merely frustrating and eliminate it. Find the friction that creates ownership and meaning, and make sure it's there.

Just add an egg.

Chapter Seven: Design Moments, Not Messages

In London, if you want to become a licensed black cab driver, you must pass an examination known simply as "the Knowledge." It's considered one of the most demanding tests in the world.

Candidates spend years, typically three to four, sometimes longer, memorising every street, landmark, hotel, restaurant, and point of interest within a six-mile radius of Charing Cross. That's approximately 25,000 streets and 100,000 landmarks. They're tested on the most efficient routes between any two points, accounting for traffic patterns, one-way systems, and time of day. The failure rate is punishing.

Here's what's interesting: the Knowledge was designed in 1865. Today, every smartphone has GPS navigation that can calculate optimal routes instantly. A driver with no local knowledge whatsoever can navigate London as efficiently as a thirty-year veteran, at least in theory. The practical case for the Knowledge has largely evaporated.

And yet it persists. Not just as a regulatory requirement, but as a source of genuine pride among cabbies and genuine respect from passengers. People choose black cabs over cheaper alternatives partly because of what the Knowledge represents. The visible investment, years of study, thousands of hours of preparation, a genuine ordeal to pass, signals something about the quality of service you'll receive.

This is the power of sunk cost as a trust signal. When someone has clearly invested significant effort into something, we assume the output must be valuable. The effort becomes evidence of seriousness.

Internal communications can learn from this. Not by making everything difficult, but by understanding that visible investment creates perceived value. How you package and deliver a message signals how important it is, and by extension, how important the audience is.

The Unboxing Effect

There's a reason "unboxing videos" became a phenomenon. Millions of people watch strangers open products they've already seen advertised. The appeal isn't the product itself. It's the experience of unwrapping it. The anticipation, the reveal, the tactile satisfaction of quality packaging.

Apple understood this decades before YouTube existed. They employ designers whose sole job is the packaging experience. The weight of the box, the resistance when you lift the lid, the precise way the device sits in its cradle, the satisfying peel of the protective film. None of this affects how the phone actually works. All of it affects how you feel about the phone before you've even turned it on.

This is the unboxing effect: how something is presented shapes how it's received, independent of its actual content.

Internal communications has its own unboxing moments. The way an announcement arrives. The format it takes. The visual presentation. The medium through which it's delivered. The context that surrounds it. All of these create an experience before people engage with the actual information.

Most organisations ignore this entirely. Communications arrive as plain emails, undifferentiated from the dozens of other messages competing for attention. Important announcements look exactly like routine updates. Strategic shifts are delivered through the same channel as expense policy reminders. There's no unboxing experience because everything comes in the same plain wrapper.

The result is that significance gets lost. When everything looks the same, nothing stands out. Employees develop a kind of format blindness. They've learned that the packaging tells them nothing about importance, so they ignore it entirely.

Consider the alternative. A major strategic announcement arrives not as an email but as a calendar invitation to a dedicated fifteen-minute briefing. Attendees receive a beautifully designed one-page summary. The briefing opens with a short video from leadership, followed by live Q&A. After the session, a physical artifact, a card, a poster, a small item, arrives at people's desks.

Same information. Radically different experience. The packaging communicates: this matters. We invested in how you receive this because we want you to receive it well. You're worth this effort.

Signalling Commitment

The Knowledge works as a trust signal because the investment is visible and verifiable. Everyone knows it takes years to complete. You can't fake it. The sunk cost is real.

Internal communications can create similar signals, though obviously at a smaller scale. The question is: what investments are visible to employees, and what do they signal?

Consider these different versions of the same announcement:

Version one: an email from "Internal Communications" with a text summary of the new strategy.

Version two: a personal email from the CEO with the same text summary.

Version three: a recorded video message from the CEO explaining the strategy.

Version four: a live all-hands where the CEO presents the strategy and takes questions in real time.

The information content might be identical across all four versions. But the perceived importance escalates dramatically. Why? Because each version represents a greater investment of leadership time and attention, and time is the resource everyone knows is scarce.

A CEO who sends an email has invested minutes. A CEO who records a video has invested perhaps an hour, including preparation and multiple takes. A CEO who stands in front of the company live, taking unscripted questions, has invested significantly more, and has also taken a risk. The live format means they can't control every word. They might face difficult questions. They're making themselves vulnerable.

That vulnerability is the signal. It says: this matters enough for me to show up in person, to face whatever questions arise, to invest my most precious resource. If I didn't believe in this, I wouldn't be here.

This is why live Q&A sessions create more trust than pre-recorded messages, even when the content is identical. It's why thoughtful follow-ups signal more than initial announcements. It's why a leader who personally responds to questions in a forum creates more engagement than one who delegates to the communications team.

The effort is visible. Therefore, the commitment is credible.

The Production Value Question

This raises a practical question: how much should you invest in production value for internal communications?

The instinct in many organisations is to default to low production value. Internal communications aren't customer-facing. Nobody expects broadcast quality. And besides, isn't there something more authentic about a simple, unpolished approach?

Sometimes yes. We'll get to counter-signalling in a moment. But the default to low production value often isn't a strategic choice. It's a failure to recognise that production value communicates meaning.

When leadership releases a slick, professionally produced video to customers and a grainy webcam recording to employees, what message does that send? When external marketing materials are beautifully designed and internal communications are plain text emails, what does that signal about the relative importance of internal and external audiences?

Employees notice these disparities, even if they don't consciously articulate them. The discrepancy tells a story: we invest in the people we're trying to impress; you are not those people.

The alternative isn't to produce broadcast-quality content for every internal message. That would be absurd. It's to be intentional about matching production value to significance. High-stakes communications deserve high-quality packaging. Routine communications can be simple. The key is that the packaging should correlate with importance, so employees can use the format itself as a signal.

The Tier Framework

Here's a practical framework for thinking about production investment.

Tier One communications are your most significant: major strategic shifts, leadership changes, reorganisations, crisis responses, annual milestones. These deserve premium treatment. Video content should be professionally shot or at least carefully produced. Written materials should be designed, not just typed. The delivery mechanism should be distinctive: a dedicated event, a special channel, something that marks this as different from routine traffic. There should be artifacts: summary documents, visual materials, things people can keep or reference.

Tier Two communications are significant but not exceptional: programme launches, policy changes, quarterly updates, project milestones. These deserve good production value but not the full premium treatment. A well-written email with thoughtful formatting. A town hall mention with proper context. A clean, branded document. Professional but not elaborate.

Tier Three communications are routine: process reminders, administrative updates, regular cadence communications. These should be clear and efficient. No frills, no apologies. The simplicity is appropriate; dressing up routine information in premium packaging would actually undermine your Tier One communications by diluting their distinctiveness.

The framework helps answer "how much should we invest?" by first answering "how significant is this?" Match the investment to the importance, and you create a visual language that employees can read. They learn that premium packaging means premium importance. The format becomes a signal they can trust.

One on the Table

There's a principle from product presentation that applies beautifully to internal communications: the power of "one on the table."

When you're trying to demonstrate quality, showing one excellent example is more effective than showing many average ones. A single beautifully crafted prototype communicates more than a hundred adequate ones. The focused attention on quality signals seriousness in a way that volume cannot.

Most internal communications operate on the opposite principle. We try to communicate comprehensively: every initiative mentioned, every achievement listed, every update included. The result is a dense, undifferentiated mass of information where nothing stands out because everything is competing for attention.

The "one on the table" approach is different. Instead of covering everything, you select one thing and present it excellently. One customer story, told with depth and detail. One project spotlight, explored thoroughly. One example of values in action, given the attention it deserves.

This doesn't mean you never communicate about other things. It means that when you want something to really land, you give it singular focus. You clear the table of everything else and let this one thing shine.

Consider how this applies to a town hall meeting. The typical approach is to pack the agenda with updates from every function: ten minutes on strategy, five minutes on finance, eight minutes on HR initiatives, six minutes on IT projects, and so on. By the end, nobody remembers any of it.

The "one on the table" approach might dedicate half the town hall to a single topic, explored in depth. A real customer story with video testimony. A genuine problem solved, with the people who solved it explaining how. Questions and discussion that go deeper than surface level. The other topics still exist, perhaps they're covered in a written summary distributed before or after, but the live experience is focused on one thing done excellently.

People leave remembering that one thing. They tell colleagues about it. It creates an impression that persists. That's the power of focus.

Counter-Signalling

Now for the twist. Sometimes less production value communicates more confidence.

Counter-signalling is a concept from economics and evolutionary biology. It describes situations where not displaying the typical signals of quality actually signals higher quality. The logic is: only someone who truly has quality can afford to not signal it.

Think about how this works in everyday life. A wealthy person might dress simply because they don't need to prove anything. The ostentatious display of wealth is for those who are insecure about their status. An expert might explain things plainly because they're not trying to impress anyone with jargon. The complex terminology is for those still establishing their credentials.

In organisational communications, counter-signalling shows up when deliberate simplicity conveys confidence better than polish.

Consider two versions of a CEO update during uncertain times:

Version one: professionally produced video, careful scripting, multiple camera angles, subtle background music, polished graphics showing key metrics.

Version two: CEO speaking directly to camera from their home office, clearly unrehearsed, occasionally pausing to find the right words, no production value whatsoever.

In stable times, version one might read as more "professional." But in a crisis, version two might actually build more trust. Why? Because the lack of production signals authenticity. The CEO isn't hiding behind polish. They're speaking directly, human to human. The roughness is the proof of genuineness.

This is counter-signalling. The absence of typical quality signals (production value) actually signals a different kind of quality (authenticity). Only a leader who genuinely has something real to say can afford to say it without the safety of professional production.

Counter-signalling works best when there's something to prove. When trust is in question. When circumstances are unusual. When you need to cut through the noise of typical corporate communications. In those moments, simplicity isn't a failure of investment. It's a strategic choice that communicates confidence and authenticity.

The key is intentionality. There's a difference between deliberately simple communication (counter-signalling) and communication that's simple because nobody could be bothered (just low quality). The former is a choice; the latter is a default. Employees can usually tell the difference.

When Polish Backfires

Let's be specific about when high production value becomes counterproductive.

During crises, polish can read as tone-deaf. When employees are worried about their jobs and a slickly produced video arrives talking about "exciting changes ahead," the dissonance is jarring. The production value suggests business as usual; the reality is anything but. In these moments, raw and direct builds more trust than polished and professional.

When authenticity is the message, production can undermine it. If you're trying to communicate that leadership is listening, that things are changing, that the organisation is becoming more human, an over-produced message contradicts the content. The medium is fighting the message. Sometimes a genuine, imperfect communication does more than a perfect one.

When speed matters, polish causes delay. If you need to respond quickly to events, waiting for production creates a gap that gets filled by rumour and speculation. A fast, simple response beats a slow, polished one. The timeliness is its own signal of seriousness.

When resources are visibly constrained, premium production raises questions. If the organisation is cutting costs, freezing hiring, or asking for sacrifice, and then a beautifully produced video arrives, employees notice the disconnect. "Where did the budget for that come from?" The production value that was meant to signal importance instead signals misplaced priorities.

The principle is: production value should be appropriate to context. Premium treatment for Tier One communications in stable times. Strategic simplicity when authenticity, speed, or sensitivity require it. The worst choice is always unintentional: defaulting to polish when simplicity would work better, or defaulting to simplicity when investment would signal importance.

The Strategy Transformation

Let me give you a concrete example of how these principles come together.

A company I worked with had a tradition: every year, the CEO presented the annual strategy at an all-company meeting. The presentation had grown over time to 47 slides. It covered everything: market analysis, competitive positioning, financial targets, strategic pillars, key initiatives, functional priorities, metrics dashboards. It was comprehensive. It was also completely forgettable. Employees sat through ninety minutes of slides and walked away with no clear sense of what actually mattered.

The communications team proposed a radical simplification. Instead of 47 slides, three minutes of video. Instead of comprehensive coverage, one clear theme. Instead of dense data, a single compelling story.

The video opened with a customer, a real customer, on camera, describing a problem they'd struggled with for years. Then a brief clip of the employee who'd solved it, explaining how. Then the CEO, connecting this story to the year's strategic focus: "This is what we're trying to do more of. This year, everything we do is in service of this."

After the video, instead of an hour of slides, thirty minutes of live discussion. What does this mean for your team? What obstacles do you see? What would help?

And then, the artifact: a physical card delivered to every employee. On one side, the customer's photo and a one-sentence summary of their story. On the other side, three questions: What's one thing you could do this month to create a moment like this? What's getting in your way? Who could you talk to about it?

Same strategy. Radically different communication. The response was unlike anything the company had experienced. People talked about the customer story for weeks. Managers used the cards in team discussions. The strategic theme, which was, in essence, the same theme as the previous year's 47-slide deck, actually stuck.

What changed? The communications team had applied the principles: intentional design, appropriate production value, singular focus, a tangible artifact, and space for dialogue rather than one-way broadcast. The strategy became a moment, not a message.

Designing for Memory

The ultimate test of a communication is whether it's remembered. Not just whether it was received, opened, or even understood in the moment, but whether it persists. Does it come to mind later? Does it influence behaviour? Does it get referenced and discussed?

Memory is selective. We don't remember everything we encounter. We remember what stands out, what's emotionally resonant, what's connected to things we already care about. Designed moments create memory in ways that routine messages don't.

When you're planning a significant communication, ask: what will people remember about this in a month? If the honest answer is "nothing in particular," you haven't designed a moment. You've just sent a message.

The elements that create memory are the elements we've been discussing: the visible investment that signals importance, the unboxing experience that creates anticipation, the singular focus that allows depth, the artifacts that persist beyond the moment, the human elements that create emotional connection.

None of this is about manipulation or tricks. It's about respecting the fact that attention is scarce, memory is selective, and communication is competing against everything else in people's lives. If something genuinely matters, it deserves to be communicated in a way that does it justice. If it doesn't matter enough to invest in properly, maybe it doesn't need to be communicated at all.

The Investment Test

Here's a final practical question to ask before any significant communication: what are we investing, and is it visible?

Investment can take many forms. Leader time: is a senior person lending their credibility and attention? Production effort: is the packaging thoughtful and appropriate? Creative energy: is this communication crafted or merely assembled? Follow-through: are we committing to engage with questions and feedback?

Whatever you're investing, make it visible. Not in a self-congratulatory way ("look how hard we worked on this"), but in a way that signals to the audience that this communication was worth doing properly. The investment is the evidence that this matters.

When the Knowledge was created in 1865, it made practical sense. There was no other way for cab drivers to learn London's streets. Today, its practical justification is thin. But its symbolic power remains. The visible investment still signals quality, commitment, and seriousness.

Your communications don't need to require years of study. But they do need to show that someone cared enough to do them well. That visible investment is what transforms a message into a moment.

PART THREE

THE PRACTICAL PLAYBOOK

Chapter Eight: Personalisation Without The Creepy

A few years ago, the American retailer Target made headlines for something their data scientists had figured out. By analysing purchasing patterns, they could predict when a customer was pregnant, often before she'd told anyone. A combination of signals, switching to unscented lotion, buying certain vitamins, purchasing larger handbags, created a predictive model that was remarkably accurate.

Target started sending targeted coupons for baby products to customers their algorithm had identified as likely pregnant. In one now-famous case, a father complained to a store manager that his teenage daughter was receiving baby-related marketing. "Are you trying to encourage her to get pregnant?" he demanded. The manager apologised profusely. A few days later, the manager called to apologise again. The father was more subdued this time. "It turns out," he said, "there's been some activities in my house I wasn't completely aware of. She's due in August."

The algorithm had outed a teenager's pregnancy to her father via coupon mailer.

This story has become a cautionary tale in marketing circles about the line between personalisation and surveillance. Target's data science was impressive. Their judgment about how to use it was catastrophic. The experience of receiving that mailer wasn't "oh, how convenient." It was "oh God, what do they know about me?"

Internal communications faces exactly the same tension. We have access to remarkable amounts of data about employees: what they've read, what they've clicked, what training they've completed, what team they're on, what their performance looks like, where they sit, how long they've been with the company. We could, in theory, use this data to create highly personalised communications.

The question is whether we should. And if so, how.

The Personalisation Spectrum

Let's start by mapping the territory. Personalisation in internal communications exists on a spectrum, from completely generic to individually targeted.

At one end, you have **mass communication.** Everyone receives the same message in the same format. There's no acknowledgment that different people might have different needs, contexts, or interests. It's simple to produce, impossible to get wrong from a privacy perspective, and almost certainly irrelevant to most recipients.

Move along the spectrum and you get **segment-based communication.** Messages are tailored to broad groups: all managers receive one version, all individual contributors another. Or communications are segmented by function, by location, by tenure. This increases relevance without requiring individual-level data.

Further along, you have **role-based personalisation.** The system knows your specific job and tailors content accordingly. A finance manager sees different information than a sales manager. A team lead in Manchester sees different details than one in Singapore. The personalisation is based on work context, not personal behaviour.

Then you have **behavioural personalisation.** The system knows what you've previously engaged with and uses that to predict what you'll want next. "Because you read last month's article on leadership, here's another one." "You haven't completed the security training, here's a reminder."

At the far end is **individual prediction.** The system infers things about you that you haven't explicitly shared. It predicts your needs before you've expressed them. It knows what you're likely to do and pre-emptively communicates accordingly.

Each step along this spectrum increases potential relevance. Each step also increases potential creepiness. The art is finding the right point on the spectrum for your organisation and your culture.

The Creepy Line

What makes personalisation feel creepy rather than helpful? It's worth understanding this precisely, because the difference isn't always obvious.

Creepiness arises when there's a gap between what you thought they knew and what they apparently know. The Target example is extreme, but the dynamic is common. You receive a communication that reveals knowledge you didn't realise the organisation had. Even if that knowledge is benign, even if the communication is genuinely helpful, the revelation creates discomfort. "Wait, they're tracking that?"

Creepiness also arises when the personalisation feels disproportionate to the relationship. A message from your direct manager that references your recent work feels normal; the manager knows your work. The same message from a corporate system that's clearly automated feels different. The intimacy is inappropriate to the relationship.

And creepiness arises when personalisation removes agency. If the system is deciding what you see based on what it thinks you want, you're no longer in control of your information diet. This can feel manipulative even when the intentions are good. "Who decided I needed to see this? Why am I being managed?"

The common thread is a violation of expected boundaries. Personalisation feels helpful when it operates within the boundaries you expect. It feels creepy when it reveals that those boundaries don't exist, when the organisation knows more than you thought, acts more intimately than the relationship warrants, or removes choices you thought you had.

Light-Touch Personalisation

So how do you increase relevance without crossing into creepy territory? The answer is what I call light-touch personalisation: using gentle cues that suggest relevance without confirming surveillance.

Consider the difference between these two messages:

Message A: *"Hi Sarah. Our records show you haven't completed the Q3 compliance training. Your completion rate is currently 67%, below the team average of 84%. Please complete the remaining modules by Friday."*

Message B: *"A reminder that Q3 compliance training is due Friday. If you've already completed it, thank you, please disregard this message. If you're still working through it, now's a good time to finish up."*

Message A is more personalised. It uses Sarah's name, references her specific completion rate, and compares her to her peers. It's also faintly menacing. The system is watching. The system knows. The system is judging.

Message B is less personalised but more humane. It acknowledges that not everyone is in the same situation without calling out exactly who is where. It gives Sarah an out if she's already completed the training. It doesn't reveal exactly what the system knows about her.

Light-touch personalisation uses phrasing like:

"You may be someone who..." Rather than "Our data shows you are..."

"If this applies to you..." Rather than "This applies to you because..."

"Some teams are finding..." Rather than "Your team specifically has..."

"For those who haven't yet..." Rather than "You haven't yet..."

These phrases suggest relevance without confirming surveillance. They allow the reader to self-identify rather than being identified. They preserve a sense of agency and privacy even when the organisation does, in fact, have data that could enable more specific targeting.

Is this less efficient than precise targeting? Perhaps marginally. But efficiency isn't the only value. Trust matters too. And light-touch personalisation preserves trust while still improving relevance.

The Opt-In Principle

The most powerful tool for personalisation without creepiness is simple: let people choose.

Opt-in personalisation inverts the typical dynamic. Instead of the organisation deciding what you should see based on data it's collected, you tell the organisation what you want to see. Instead of being profiled, you're empowered.

This can work in several ways.

Topic tracks let employees subscribe to the content areas that matter to them. Interested in leadership development? Subscribe to that track. Want updates on sustainability initiatives? Opt in. Don't care about the social committee's events? Opt out. The personalisation is explicit and chosen, not inferred and imposed.

Preference settings let employees control format and frequency. Do you want a daily digest or weekly summary? Email notifications or app alerts? Full articles or headlines only? These choices feel like service, not surveillance.

Interest declarations invite people to share context that helps communications be more relevant. "I'm interested in international opportunities." "I'm curious about technical career paths." "I'd like to hear more about our work with specific clients." This information is volunteered, not extracted.

The psychology here is important. When you choose to share information, it doesn't feel like surveillance when that information is used. It feels like responsiveness. The organisation is giving you what you asked for. That's service, not creepiness.

Opt-in systems do require effort to set up and maintain. They require employees to actually make choices, which some won't bother to do. They're less comprehensive than systems that profile everyone automatically. But they build trust rather than eroding it. And in the long run, trust matters more than targeting precision.

Cultural Calibration

Perceptions of privacy and personalisation vary significantly across cultures. What feels helpful in one context feels intrusive in another. Any global organisation needs to calibrate its approach accordingly.

Some cultures have stronger expectations of privacy boundaries. Communications that reference individual behaviour or performance may feel appropriate in some contexts and deeply uncomfortable in others. The directness that works in one office may come across as confrontational elsewhere.

Some cultures have different relationships with hierarchy and authority. A personal message from the CEO might feel inspiring in one market and suspicious in another. "Why is the CEO writing to me specifically? What have I done wrong?"

Some cultures have different norms around public recognition. Calling out an individual for praise in front of peers is motivating in some contexts and embarrassing in others. What's intended as celebration can land as unwanted exposure.

The implication is that personalisation strategies can't be global by default. They need local calibration. This might mean different approaches in different regions, or it might mean defaulting to lighter-touch personalisation that works across contexts.

When in doubt, err toward privacy. It's better to leave some relevance on the table than to cross a cultural line you didn't know existed. You can always increase personalisation based on feedback. It's much harder to rebuild trust after you've violated it.

Milestone Celebrations Done Right

One of the most common uses of personalisation in internal communications is celebrating milestones: work anniversaries, project completions, promotions, retirements. These are natural moments for individual recognition.

They're also moments where personalisation frequently goes wrong.

The failure mode usually looks like this: an automated system generates a "personal" message that is obviously automated. "Congratulations on your five-year anniversary! We appreciate your contributions to [COMPANY NAME]." The message is technically personalised, it has your name and the correct milestone, but it feels generic because it clearly is generic. A machine generated it. No human thought about you specifically.

This is worse than no recognition at all. It highlights that the organisation could have celebrated you personally but chose instead to automate. The efficiency is visible, and what it signals is: you weren't worth the effort of a real message.

Milestone celebrations that work have human fingerprints on them. This doesn't mean every message must be individually handwritten, that doesn't scale. But it means the human element should be visible and genuine.

Some approaches that work:

Manager-mediated recognition. The system prompts the manager that a milestone is approaching. The manager writes a personal note that's delivered through the system. The automation is in the prompting, not the recognition itself.

Team-sourced celebration. For significant milestones, invite teammates to contribute a sentence or two of appreciation. Compile these into a single message. The automation is in the aggregation, but the content is genuinely personal.

Specific appreciation. If you must automate, make the content specific. Instead of generic appreciation for "contributions," reference actual work: "Congratulations on five years, a journey that's included the product launch in 2021, the client recovery that saved the Morrison account, and the team you've built in the Birmingham office." This requires data, but it's data used to demonstrate genuine attention, not to profile behaviour.

Thoughtful artifacts. A personalised video compilation. A small gift that reflects something about the person. A donation to a charity they care about. These signals of effort communicate value in ways that templated messages cannot.

The principle is: if you're going to personalise, make it count. A light-touch generic message might be better than a poorly executed "personal" one. But a genuinely thoughtful personal recognition beats both.

When Personalisation Backfires

Let me share some examples of personalisation that went wrong, so you can learn from others' mistakes.

The surveillance reveal. An organisation implemented a system that tracked which internal communications employees had opened. They then sent targeted reminders to people who hadn't read important messages. The intentions were good, ensuring critical information reached everyone, but the effect was chilling. Employees felt monitored. Open rates actually dropped as people started ignoring all communications in protest.

The over-specific reference. A manager received an automated prompt to recognise an employee's work anniversary. The prompt included data about the employee's recent performance metrics, which the manager referenced in their "personal" note. The employee was disturbed to discover their manager had such specific surveillance data at their fingertips. The recognition felt less like celebration than assessment.

The tone-deaf celebration. An organisation automated work anniversary messages with cheerful language. An employee going through a difficult period, dealing with health issues and considering leaving, received a bubbly message about "all the wonderful memories" they'd surely created. The dissonance between the message's assumed sentiment and the employee's actual experience felt mocking.

The public exposure. A company celebrated high performers by automatically posting their achievements to an internal social feed. Some employees were delighted. Others were mortified by the unsolicited public attention. Some felt the data behind the recognition was questionable and didn't want to be associated with metrics they couldn't control.

The pattern across these failures is the same: personalisation was implemented as a system feature without sufficient thought about the human experience of receiving it. The technology worked perfectly. The judgment was absent.

A Style Guide for Privacy-Safe Personalisation

Based on everything we've discussed, here's a practical style guide for personalising internal communications without crossing lines.

Principle one: suggest rather than assert. Use language that implies relevance without confirming data collection. "You might be interested in..." not "Based on your reading history..." "If you're in a customer-facing role..." not "Our records show you're in a customer-facing role..."

Principle two: offer choices, not prescriptions. "You can customise your preferences at any time" should be more than a legal footer. It should be a genuine invitation. Make it easy to control what communications you receive and how you receive them.

Principle three: acknowledge uncertainty. "If this doesn't apply to you, please disregard" is a simple phrase that respects individual circumstances. It acknowledges that systems don't have perfect information about people's lives.

Principle four: keep humans in the loop for sensitive moments. Milestones, life events, and difficult conversations shouldn't be fully automated. Use systems to prompt and support human communication, not replace it.

Principle five: be transparent about data use. If you're using data to personalise communications, say so, and say what data you're using. "This message was sent to all people managers" is more trustworthy than a message that's been silently targeted.

Principle six: test for creepiness. Before deploying personalised communications, ask: if I received this message, would I feel helped or surveilled? Would I think "that's useful" or "that's unsettling"? Trust your instincts, and err toward caution.

Principle seven: calibrate for culture. Recognise that different teams, functions, regions, and generations may have different comfort levels with personalisation. What works for digital-native employees in a tech company may not work for everyone. Build in flexibility.

The Trust Trade-Off

Here's the fundamental tension: personalisation done well increases relevance, which increases engagement, which increases effectiveness. But personalisation done poorly erodes trust, which undermines everything else.

The trade-off isn't between personalised and generic. It's between trust-building personalisation and trust-eroding personalisation. The former respects boundaries, offers choices, and keeps humans visible in the process. The latter treats employees as data points to be optimised, reveals surveillance that feels disproportionate, and automates moments that should be human.

Most organisations haven't thought carefully about where they want to be on this spectrum. They implement the personalisation features their technology vendors offer without asking whether those features are appropriate for their culture. They optimise for engagement metrics without considering the trust costs.

The organisations that get this right are intentional. They define what personalisation means for them. They draw explicit lines about what data they will and won't use. They test with employees before rolling out widely. They measure trust alongside engagement.

Personalisation is powerful. Used well, it makes communications more relevant, more valued, and more effective. Used poorly, it makes the organisation feel like a surveillance system that happens to employ people.

The difference is judgment, not technology. The tools can do almost anything. The question is what they should do.

Chapter Nine: Support At The Point Of Need

Here's something that should be obvious but apparently isn't: the purpose of internal communications is not to send messages. It's to create understanding and enable action.

Most organisations measure the sending part obsessively. Open rates, click-through rates, reach, frequency, channel coverage. They've optimised the machinery of distribution to a fine degree. They can tell you exactly how many people opened the email, at what time, on which device.

What they can't tell you is what happened next.

Did people understand the message? Did they have questions? Were those questions answered? Did they encounter obstacles when trying to act? Did they give up? Did they find workarounds? Did they complain to colleagues? Did they lose a little more trust in the organisation's ability to communicate clearly?

The gap between "message sent" and "outcome achieved" is where most internal communications fail. And it's almost entirely unmeasured, unmanaged, and unresourced.

This chapter is about what happens after you hit send. It's about the support infrastructure that turns communication into comprehension and comprehension into action. It's about investing where failure actually hurts.

The Bottom of the Funnel

In marketing, there's a concept called the funnel. At the top, you have awareness: people who know your product exists. In the middle, you have consideration: people who are evaluating whether to buy. At the bottom, you have conversion: people who actually make a purchase.

Sophisticated marketers know that optimising the bottom of the funnel often yields better returns than optimising the top. It doesn't matter how many people are aware of your product if they all abandon their shopping carts at checkout. A small improvement in conversion rate can be worth more than a large improvement in awareness.

Internal communications has its own funnel, though we rarely think of it that way.

At the top: people who receive the communication.

In the middle: people who read it, understand it, and know what's expected of them.

At the bottom: people who successfully take action, get their questions answered, and move forward without friction.

Where do most internal communications teams focus their energy? The top of the funnel. Sending messages, reaching audiences, achieving coverage. Where does failure actually hurt? The bottom. The person who read the announcement, had a question, couldn't find anyone to ask, and gave up. The team that tried to implement the new process, encountered an edge case, got no response when they raised it, and went back to the old way. The manager who wanted to support the change but couldn't get answers to their team's concerns.

Every one of these failures erodes trust. Every one makes the next communication harder. And almost none of them show up in your metrics.

The Hidden Phone Number Problem

Let me tell you about a pattern I've seen in organisation after organisation. I call it the hidden phone number problem.

A major change is announced. The communication is clear about what's changing and why. It includes a link to an FAQ. It says "if you have questions, please reach out."

Reach out to whom?

Sometimes there's no contact information at all, just a vague invitation to ask questions somewhere, somehow. Sometimes there's a generic email address that goes to a shared inbox monitored by no one in particular. Sometimes there's a named contact, but they're the wrong person, a communications manager who can't answer substantive questions about the change itself.

And sometimes, this is the one that really gets me, there's a phone number, but you have to click through three links and scroll to the bottom of a sub-page to find it. It's technically available. It's practically hidden.

The message this sends is clear: we don't really want you to contact us. We've met the legal requirement of providing a way to reach us, but we've made it hard enough that most people won't bother. Questions are a burden. You're on your own.

Compare this to what good support looks like. A named person, not a role, a person, who owns the communication and is available to answer questions. Multiple channels to reach them: email, phone, Slack, office hours. Fast response times: questions answered within hours, not days. Visible commitment: "I'm here to help you with this. Here's how to reach me. I'll respond within four hours during business hours."

The difference isn't resources. Putting a name and phone number in a communication costs nothing. Committing to response times costs attention, not money. The difference is philosophy. Do you see questions as a burden to be minimised or as signals to be valued?

The Human Back-Stop

Every significant communication should have a human back-stop: a real person who stands behind it and takes ownership of ensuring it lands.

This doesn't mean one person answers every question. For large-scale changes, that's not practical. It means one person is visibly accountable, coordinates the support response, and ensures nothing falls through the cracks.

The human back-stop has several components.

A named owner. Someone whose name is attached to the communication and who is publicly responsible for it. This person doesn't have to be senior. In fact, for practical reasons, they probably shouldn't be. But they need to have enough authority to get answers and enough bandwidth to respond.

Visible contact information. Not hidden in a FAQ. Not buried in a sub-page. Right there in the communication: "Questions? Contact Sarah Chen at sarah.chen@company.com or on Slack at @schen. I'm holding office hours on Thursday at 2pm if you'd prefer to talk live."

A clear escalation path. Sarah can't answer everything. Some questions will require input from legal, finance, or senior leadership. The back-stop includes a mechanism for escalating questions that need it, and a commitment to come back with answers rather than letting questions disappear into the void.

Defined response times. "I'll respond within four hours during business hours" or "Expect an answer within one business day." The specific commitment matters less than having one. It sets expectations and creates accountability.

A feedback loop. Questions that come in should inform future communications. If the same question comes up repeatedly, that's a signal that the original communication was unclear. The back-stop doesn't just answer questions. They collect intelligence about what's working and what isn't.

This sounds like a lot of work. It is, for significant communications. But most organisations are already doing this work. They're just doing it invisibly and inefficiently. Questions get asked through informal channels. Managers scramble to find answers. Rumours spread while people wait. The human back-stop doesn't create work; it makes existing work visible and effective.

Channel Choice and Autonomy

One of the most robust findings in customer service research is that offering choice improves satisfaction, even when people choose the objectively worse option.

Customers who choose to wait on hold are less frustrated than customers forced to wait on hold, even for the same duration. The choice creates a sense of control. The wait becomes something you opted into rather than something imposed on you.

The same dynamic applies to internal support. People have different preferences for how they get help. Some want to ask questions in writing and receive written answers they can refer back to. Some want to talk to a human being in real time. Some want the anonymity of a question submitted to a general inbox. Some want the directness of a named contact.

Offering multiple channels respects these differences. It says: we recognise you're an individual with your own preferences, and we've designed support to accommodate you.

Practical channel options might include:

Written channels: a dedicated email address, a form submission, a Slack channel or Teams space where questions can be posted.

Synchronous channels: office hours where people can drop in with questions, scheduled one-on-one time with the back-stop owner, a phone number for urgent issues.

Peer channels: a space where employees can answer each other's questions, with the back-stop monitoring and correcting misinformation.

Self-service channels: an FAQ that actually answers frequently asked questions, a searchable knowledge base, a decision tree for common scenarios.

Not every communication needs all of these. A routine policy update might need only a FAQ and an email contact. A major reorganisation might need the full suite. The principle is to offer appropriate choice, not to build identical infrastructure for every message.

The hidden benefit of channel choice is that it generates data. When you see which channels people use, you learn something about their needs. If everyone's choosing office hours over written FAQs, that suggests the FAQ isn't answering their real questions. If the phone line is getting heavy traffic, that suggests people need more reassurance than written communication can provide.

Response Time as a Signal

How long it takes you to answer questions says something about how much you care. This is true even when the delay is perfectly reasonable and people intellectually understand the reasons for it.

Fast responses signal: this matters to us. You matter to us. We're taking this seriously.

Slow responses signal: you're not a priority. We've moved on. Figure it out yourself.

This isn't entirely fair. Sometimes questions require research. Sometimes the right person is on holiday. Sometimes there are genuine reasons for delay. But fairness isn't the point. Perception is. And the perception created by slow responses is corrosive.

The solution isn't to answer every question instantly. That's not possible. The solution is to acknowledge quickly even when you can't answer quickly.

"Thanks for your question. I'm looking into this and will get back to you by tomorrow" is a response. It takes thirty seconds to send. It communicates that the question was received, that someone is working on it, and when to expect an answer. It transforms uncertain waiting into certain waiting, exactly the principle we discussed in Chapter Five.

Some organisations set explicit service levels for internal communications support. Questions acknowledged within two hours. Substantive response within one business day. Complex questions requiring escalation within three business days. These commitments create accountability and set expectations.

The commitments should be realistic. There's no point promising what you can't deliver. But they should also be ambitious enough to signal genuine responsiveness. "We'll get back to you within two weeks" is technically a commitment, but it signals that you're not prioritising support.

Investing Where Failure Hurts

Let's step back and think about resource allocation.

Most internal communications teams are under-resourced. There's always more to communicate than there's capacity to communicate it. Choices must be made.

The default choice is to invest in production: creating more communications, more campaigns, more content. This feels productive. It's visible. You can point to what you've made.

But if your communications aren't landing, if people don't understand, can't act, get stuck without support, then producing more communications just compounds the problem. You're adding to the noise without improving the signal.

The alternative is to invest in support: ensuring the communications you do send actually work. This means fewer, better-supported messages rather than more, unsupported ones.

Consider the maths. You send a communication to 5,000 employees. Ten percent have questions. That's 500 questions. If half of those people give up without asking because support is too hard to access, that's 250 employees who are now confused, frustrated, or working around the change. If the other half do ask but wait three days for a response, that's 250 employees spending three days in uncertainty, possibly spreading misinformation, definitely losing trust.

Now imagine you invested in robust support. You answer questions within hours. You surface common questions and proactively address them. You make it easy for people to get help. The same communication now lands with the same 5,000 employees, but outcomes are completely different.

The second scenario required more investment in support and possibly less investment in the next communication. But the overall effectiveness is dramatically higher.

This is what I mean by investing where failure hurts. A communication that's perfectly crafted but poorly supported is worth less than a communication that's adequately crafted and excellently supported. The support infrastructure is where the outcome is determined.

The Repeat Question Signal

Here's a metric that almost nobody tracks but everyone should: repeat questions.

When the same question comes up multiple times, that's a signal. It might mean the original communication was unclear. It might mean there's a gap in the FAQ. It might mean there's an edge case you hadn't anticipated. Whatever the cause, the repeat question is information.

Tracking repeat questions requires categorising and counting questions as they come in. This takes effort, but it's not complicated. A simple spreadsheet can capture: question received, date, category, answer provided, resolution time. Review weekly. Look for patterns.

The patterns tell you what to do. If "how do I access the new system?" is coming up repeatedly, your access instructions aren't clear enough. If "what happens if I'm part-time?" keeps appearing, you haven't addressed that scenario. If "who approved this?" is a frequent question, you haven't established sufficient legitimacy.

These insights should feed back into your communications. Update the FAQ. Send a follow-up clarification. Add a section to the next announcement that proactively addresses the common questions.

The goal is to reduce repeat questions over time. Each cycle of communication should be informed by what you learned from supporting the last one. The support infrastructure becomes a learning system, not just a response system.

The Service Level Agreement

For organisations that want to formalise their approach to communication support, a service level agreement can be useful.

This doesn't need to be a bureaucratic document. It's a clear statement of what support you commit to providing and what response times you commit to meeting.

A simple service level might include:

Coverage: what communications have dedicated support and what's the baseline for everything else.

Channels: what ways people can get help and when each channel is staffed.

Response times: how quickly different types of questions will be acknowledged and answered.

Escalation: how questions beyond the front-line team's authority will be handled.

Feedback loop: how insights from support will inform future communications.

Publishing this service level, making it visible to employees, creates accountability and sets expectations. People know what to expect and can hold the communications team to their commitments.

It also creates internal clarity. When the team knows they've committed to responding within four hours, they organise their work accordingly. The commitment shapes behaviour.

After the Send

Let me close this chapter with a reframe.

Most internal communications teams think their job is done when the communication goes out. The work is in the crafting, the approvals, the production, the distribution. Send is the finish line.

But for the audience, the employees who receive the communication, send is the start line. That's when they encounter the message, form their understanding, decide what to do, encounter obstacles, have questions, need support.

The best internal communications teams understand this. They think of send not as the end of their work but as the beginning of a different kind of work. The support phase. The landing phase. The "did it actually work?" phase.

This doesn't mean infinite resources dedicated to every communication. It means intentional investment in the infrastructure that helps communications land: visible contacts, multiple channels, fast response times, feedback loops, learning systems.

It means measuring what happens after send, not just what happens until send.

It means recognising that a communication that's sent but doesn't land is worse than useless. It's consumed resources, created noise, and failed to achieve its purpose. The only thing worse than not communicating is communicating badly.

Support at the point of need is how you ensure you're not just sending messages into the void. It's how you complete the communication, not at send, but at understanding.

Chapter Ten: Pilots, Scarcity, And The Power Of Social Proof

In 1999, Google was a tiny search engine competing against established giants like Yahoo, AltaVista, and Lycos. They had no marketing budget to speak of. What they had was a strategy that would become legendary in Silicon Valley: they made Gmail invite-only.

When Gmail launched in 2004, you couldn't just sign up. You needed an invitation from someone who already had an account. Each user received a limited number of invites to share. The artificial scarcity created frenzy. People sold Gmail invites on eBay. Having a Gmail address became a status symbol. The waiting list grew into the millions.

Gmail wasn't better because it was scarce. But scarcity made people believe it was better. The exclusivity signalled quality. If they're limiting access, it must be worth limiting. If my friend had to use one of their precious invites on me, this must be something special.

This is the psychology that internal communications consistently fails to exploit. We default to broad rollouts, mass announcements, mandatory participation. Everyone gets everything, all at once, whether they want it or not. And then we wonder why nothing feels special and adoption is a grind.

There's another way. It involves pilots, scarcity, and the strategic deployment of social proof. It's slower at the start and faster in the end. It's counterintuitive, and it works.

The Pilot Paradox

Here's a paradox that every programme manager should understand: launching to everyone at once is the slow way to scale.

It seems logical that broader is faster. If you need 10,000 people to adopt something, launching to all 10,000 simultaneously should get you there quicker than starting with 100, then 500, then 2,000, then everyone else.

But this logic ignores how adoption actually works.

When you launch broadly, you spread your support resources thin. Questions overwhelm the help desk. Edge cases multiply. Problems that could have been caught early become systemic failures. Early adopters have bad experiences and tell their colleagues. Sceptics feel validated. The narrative becomes "this doesn't work" before you've had a chance to make it work.

When you launch narrowly, a true pilot with a limited group, you concentrate your resources where they matter. Every participant gets excellent support. Problems are caught and fixed before they scale. Early adopters have good experiences and become advocates. The narrative becomes "this works, and I've seen it" before sceptics have a chance to poison the well.

The pilot paradox is that limiting your initial scope actually accelerates overall adoption. The time you "lose" by starting small is more than recovered by the momentum you build.

Consider the maths. A broad launch to 10,000 people with mediocre support might achieve 40% adoption after six months: 4,000 active users, 6,000 resisters who've had bad experiences or heard bad stories. A pilot launch to 500 people with excellent support might achieve 90% adoption in that group after two months: 450 advocates who are now telling stories, answering questions, and demonstrating success. When you expand from there, you're not starting from zero. You're starting from 450 people who are actively helping you succeed.

This is why the best change management professionals are almost fanatically committed to pilots. Not because they're cautious, but because they understand that pilots are the fastest path to scale.

Social Proof Inside Organisations

The Gmail invite strategy worked because of social proof: the psychological principle that we look to others to determine what's correct, valuable, or desirable. If other people want something, it must be worth wanting. If people I respect are doing something, it must be worth doing.

Social proof operates powerfully inside organisations, though it's rarely leveraged strategically.

When a respected colleague says "I've been using the new system and it's actually better," that carries more weight than any official communication. When a team known for their scepticism adopts a new process, others take notice. When the person who always complains about change initiatives says "this one's different," people listen.

This is peer advocacy, and it's more influential than top-down messaging for most types of change. Leadership endorsement matters for legitimacy, but peer endorsement matters for credibility. Leadership can say "we believe in this." Peers can say "I've tried it and it works."

The implication for pilots is significant. Who you include in your pilot matters as much as how you run it. The goal isn't just to test the initiative. It's to create advocates who will influence the broader rollout.

Strategic pilot selection considers several factors:

Influence: who do others look to for cues about what to adopt? This isn't just formal leaders; it's the informal opinion-shapers, the people whose views carry weight.

Diversity: can you include people from different functions, locations, and levels? Advocates who represent different parts of the organisation are more effective than advocates who all look the same.

Credibility: are there known sceptics you could include? Converting a sceptic creates a more powerful advocate than confirming a believer. "Even Sarah thinks it's good, and she hates everything" is a compelling testimonial.

Connectivity: who will actually talk about their experience? Some people are natural sharers; others keep things to themselves. Prioritise people who will spread the word.

The point isn't to stack the pilot with friendly faces who'll say nice things regardless. It's to select participants whose genuine positive experience will be seen and heard by the people you need to reach next.

One Excellent Example

We covered the "one on the table" principle in Chapter Seven, but it's worth revisiting here in the context of pilots and scaling.

When you're trying to build belief in something new, one excellent example is worth more than a hundred adequate ones. A single team that's achieved remarkable results with the new process. A single department where the new system has transformed how they work. A single pilot site where adoption is near-universal and satisfaction is high.

This runs counter to the instinct to showcase breadth. "Look how many teams are using it!" feels like a stronger argument than "Look at this one team." But breadth signals scale, not quality. One excellent example signals that excellence is possible, and that's what sceptics need to see.

The psychology here relates to what researchers call the "identifiable victim effect." We respond more strongly to a single, vivid example than to statistics about many cases. A story about one team's transformation is more compelling than data about average improvements across fifty teams.

When designing pilots, optimise for creating at least one extraordinary success story. This might mean selecting a pilot group that's particularly well-positioned to succeed. It might mean concentrating support resources to ensure exceptional outcomes. It might mean extending the pilot timeline to allow for genuine transformation rather than superficial adoption.

The story you'll tell matters more than the average result you'll achieve. One team that went from struggling to thriving is worth more, rhetorically, than twenty teams that went from adequate to slightly better.

Before and After

The most compelling format for pilot stories is the before-and-after narrative. Here's where they started. Here's what changed. Here's where they are now.

Before-and-after works because it makes transformation visible. It's not enough to say "the new system is great." You need to show the contrast with what came before. The struggle makes the success meaningful.

A strong before-and-after story includes:

The starting point: what was life like before the change? Be specific and honest about the problems. "The team was spending four hours a week on manual reconciliation. Errors were common. Nobody trusted the numbers."

The transition: what was it like to adopt the new approach? Acknowledge the difficulty. "The first two weeks were rough. The interface was unfamiliar, and people kept reverting to old habits. There was grumbling."

The breakthrough: when did things click? What made the difference? "Around week three, people started seeing the time savings. When we closed the month in two days instead of five, the complaints stopped."

The outcome: where are things now? Quantify where possible. "Manual reconciliation is down to thirty minutes a week. Error rate has dropped by 80%. The finance team actually trusts our numbers for the first time."

The human element: how do people feel? "There's less stress at month-end. People go home on time. The team lead told me it's changed how she thinks about what's possible."

This structure creates a complete narrative arc: struggle, challenge, breakthrough, transformation. It's a story people can remember and retell, not just a claim they have to take on faith.

Participant Testimonials

Pilot participants are your best salespeople for the broader rollout. Their testimonials, captured and deployed strategically, do work that official communications cannot.

But not all testimonials are equal. A generic "I really like the new system" does little. A specific, credible testimonial does a lot.

Effective testimonials have several characteristics:

Specificity: concrete details about what changed and how. "I used to spend my Friday afternoons on expense reports. Now I do them in fifteen minutes on Monday morning."

Credibility: acknowledgment of initial scepticism or difficulty. "I'll be honest, I didn't think this would work. I've seen too many of these initiatives come and go. But this one's different."

Relatability: coming from someone the audience identifies with. A testimonial from someone in the same role, facing the same challenges, carries more weight than one from someone in a different context.

Emotion: how does it feel, not just what happened? "It sounds small, but not dreading month-end has made a real difference to my job satisfaction."

When collecting testimonials from pilot participants, don't just ask "what did you think?" Ask specific questions that elicit useful responses:

"What were you most worried about before we started?"

"What surprised you about the experience?"

"What would you tell a colleague who's sceptical?"

"What's specifically different about your work now?"

"What would you go back and tell yourself at the beginning?"

These questions prompt stories, not evaluations. And stories are what you need.

The Scarcity Lever

Back to Gmail's invite-only strategy. The scarcity wasn't just about managing server load. It was about creating desire through exclusivity.

Internal communications can use the same lever, though it requires a mindset shift. Instead of "everyone must participate," consider "participation is limited."

This works particularly well for discretionary initiatives: new tools, development programmes, optional training, innovation initiatives. Things where participation is a choice, not a requirement.

Compare these two framings:

Framing A: *"We're launching a new collaboration tool. All employees will receive login credentials next week. Mandatory training sessions are scheduled throughout the month."*

Framing B: *"We're piloting a new collaboration tool with a small group before wider rollout. We have 200 spots available for the initial cohort. If you'd like to be among the first to try it, register your interest by Friday."*

Same tool. Completely different psychology. Framing A positions the tool as an imposition. Framing B positions it as an opportunity.

Scarcity reframes participation from burden to privilege. It creates competition for access rather than resistance to adoption. It attracts the most motivated early adopters, exactly the people you want in your pilot, rather than forcing reluctant participants who'll drag down the experience for everyone.

This doesn't work for everything. Compliance training can't be optional. Organisation-wide system changes can't be selective. But for anything where you have discretion, scarcity is a lever worth pulling.

The Exclusive First Look

A related technique is the "exclusive first look": inviting a select group to preview something before it's widely available.

This works even when the eventual rollout will be universal. You're not making the thing scarce permanently; you're making early access scarce. The preview group gets to see it first, influence its development, and be ready to help when broader rollout happens.

The exclusive first look achieves several things simultaneously:

It creates buy-in through involvement. People who see something early feel ownership. They were consulted. Their input mattered. They're invested in the outcome.

It identifies issues before scale. The preview group will find problems you missed. Better to discover them with fifty people than five thousand.

It builds advocates. Preview participants become knowledgeable guides for their colleagues. When the broader launch happens, there are already people who can answer questions and demonstrate value.

It generates anticipation. If the preview group is talking about what they've seen, which they will, others become curious. The official launch arrives to an audience that's already interested rather than indifferent.

The invitation matters. "You're invited to an exclusive first look" is different from "We'd like your feedback on a draft." Both might involve the same activity, but the framing creates different psychological responses.

Timing the Rollout

Pilots are not ends in themselves. The goal is eventual scale. But the timing and sequencing of expansion matters enormously.

Expand too quickly, before the pilot has generated advocates and stories, and you lose the benefits of starting small. Expand too slowly, and momentum stalls, attention moves elsewhere, and the pilot becomes a permanent exception rather than a precursor to change.

The right timing depends on several factors:

Have you achieved demonstrable success? The pilot should have results worth talking about before you expand. If outcomes are ambiguous, you're not ready.

Do you have advocates ready to help? Pilot participants who can support the next cohort, answer questions, and demonstrate value. If your pilot participants aren't enthusiastic, you have a problem to solve before you scale.

Have you addressed the major issues? Problems surfaced in the pilot should be fixed before expansion. Scaling known problems just creates larger problems.

Is there demand? Are people asking when they can participate? If there's pull from outside the pilot, that's a signal to expand. If there's no interest, either your pilot isn't generating visible success or the underlying offering isn't compelling.

A staged rollout typically works better than a single jump from pilot to full scale. Pilot, then early adopter cohort, then mainstream rollout, then late adopters. This gives you multiple opportunities to learn, adjust, and build momentum.

Each stage should have its own communication strategy. What you say to early adopters is different from what you say to the mainstream is different from what you say to late adopters. Early adopters want to hear about innovation and opportunity. The mainstream wants to hear about proven results and peer success. Late adopters want to hear about simplicity and support.

The Well-Storied Pilot

Let me pull this together into a framework for what I call a "well-storied pilot": a pilot designed from the start to generate the narratives you'll need for scaling.

Phase one: selection. Choose participants strategically for influence, diversity, credibility, and connectivity. Frame participation as an opportunity, not an obligation.

Phase two: preparation. Set expectations with participants. They're not just users. They're partners in building something. Their experience will shape how this rolls out. Their feedback matters. Their stories will be heard.

Phase three: support. Resource the pilot heavily. Make it impossible to fail for reasons of inadequate support. You want to test the initiative, not the support infrastructure.

Phase four: documentation. Capture stories throughout, not just at the end. Before-and-after data. Testimonials. Specific examples of problems solved and value created. Photos and videos if appropriate.

Phase five: celebration. Mark the pilot's completion. Recognise participants. Share results visibly, both internally and with the broader organisation that will come next.

Phase six: storytelling. Deploy the stories you've captured in service of the broader rollout. Participant testimonials in launch communications. Before-and-after examples in training materials. Advocates available to answer questions.

The pilot is successful not just when participants adopt the change, but when their adoption creates the conditions for successful scaling. The stories are the output, as much as the results.

The Patience Requirement

I'll end with a note of realism. This approach requires patience.

Starting with a pilot, building advocacy, staging the rollout: this takes longer than announcing to everyone simultaneously. In organisations under pressure to show results quickly, the pilot approach can feel indulgent.

But consider the alternative. A rushed broad launch that achieves 30% adoption and generates widespread frustration. A change initiative that becomes synonymous with poor implementation. Years of lingering resistance because first impressions were bad.

The patience required for a well-run pilot is measured in weeks or months. The cost of a failed broad launch is measured in years: years of resistance, years of workarounds, years of "remember when they tried that?" stories that poison future initiatives.

Gmail could have launched to everyone in 2004. They chose artificial scarcity instead. Two decades later, it's one of the most widely used email services in the world. The slow start created the conditions for fast scaling.

Your internal initiatives operate on a smaller scale, but the principle is the same. Start small. Build belief. Let the stories spread. Then scale on a foundation of advocacy rather than resistance.

It's slower at the start. It's faster in the end.

Chapter Eleven: Showcasing The Craft

There's a restaurant in Tokyo where the chef prepares your meal in front of you. Not a teppanyaki grill with theatrical knife work. Something more understated. A small counter, perhaps eight seats, where you watch as ingredients are selected, prepared, and assembled into dishes that arrive moments later.

The food is extraordinary. But here's what's interesting: studies suggest it would taste slightly less extraordinary if you hadn't watched it being made.

This is the IKEA effect's cousin: the principle that we value things more when we can see the effort that went into creating them. The watching isn't incidental to the experience; it's central to it. The visible craft creates perceived value.

Internal communications rarely shows its work. Decisions appear fully formed. Initiatives arrive as finished products. Policies emerge from somewhere, legal, HR, leadership, with no indication of the thought, debate, and consideration that shaped them.

This invisibility is a missed opportunity. When employees see the craft behind decisions, they're more likely to accept trade-offs, extend patience, and trust that someone competent is in charge. When they don't see the craft, they're left to assume the worst: that decisions were arbitrary, unconsidered, or made by people who don't understand the reality on the ground.

This chapter is about strategic transparency: showing enough of the work to build trust, without showing so much that you undermine confidence or create confusion.

The "How It's Made" Principle

There's a television programme called "How It's Made" that's been running for over two decades. Each episode shows the manufacturing process behind everyday objects: golf balls, aluminium foil, saxophones, potato chips. It's oddly compelling. Millions of people have watched episodes about products they have no intention of buying, made by processes they'll never use.

Why? Because seeing how something is made creates appreciation for it. The golf ball you ignored becomes interesting when you understand the seventeen steps required to produce it. The aluminium foil you took for granted becomes impressive when you see the engineering involved.

The same principle applies to organisational decisions. A policy that seems arbitrary becomes reasonable when you understand the constraints that shaped it. A decision that seems wrong becomes defensible when you see the alternatives that were considered and rejected.

"How it's made" content for internal communications might include:

The options considered. "We looked at three approaches: A, B, and C. Here's why we chose B." This immediately elevates the decision from "they decided" to "they considered and decided." The rigour is visible.

The constraints acknowledged. "We would have preferred X, but regulatory requirements, budget limitations, and timing constraints meant we had to adapt." This shows that decisions aren't made in a vacuum. There are real limitations being navigated.

The trade-offs explained. "This approach prioritises speed over customisation. We know that's a trade-off, and here's why we think it's the right one for now." This demonstrates that downsides were considered, not ignored.

The people involved. "This recommendation comes from a working group that included frontline managers, technical experts, and HR. Here's who was in the room." This humanises the decision and shows that diverse perspectives were included.

The iteration visible. "This is actually version three. The first version had problems X and Y, which we discovered in testing. Here's how we addressed them." This shows responsiveness and learning, not stubbornness.

None of this requires extensive documentation or elaborate transparency initiatives. It's about adding a paragraph or two to communications that would otherwise present decisions as fait accompli.

Justified Trade-Offs

Every significant decision involves trade-offs. You can't optimise for everything simultaneously. Speed conflicts with thoroughness. Standardisation conflicts with flexibility. Cost savings conflict with service levels.

Most organisations hide these trade-offs. They present decisions as unambiguously positive, as if there were no downsides at all. "We're excited to announce our new streamlined process!" without acknowledging that some teams will now have less autonomy. "We're investing in modern technology!" without mentioning the learning curve and temporary productivity dip.

This hiding backfires. Employees aren't stupid. They can see the trade-offs even when you don't name them. And when you don't name them, you signal either that you don't understand them (incompetence) or that you're deliberately concealing them (dishonesty). Neither interpretation builds trust.

The alternative is to name and justify the trade-offs explicitly.

"This decision prioritises consistency across regions over local flexibility. We know that means some regional teams will lose autonomy they valued. Here's why we think the benefits of consistency outweigh that cost, and here's what we're doing to preserve local input where it matters most."

"Moving to this vendor will save significant money, which we need given budget pressures. The trade-off is that their support isn't as comprehensive as our current provider. Here's how we're mitigating that, and here's our commitment to revisit if service levels drop."

"We're accelerating the timeline, which means we're accepting more risk than we'd normally prefer. We've decided speed is more important in this case because of competitive pressures. Here's what we're doing to manage the risk, and here's our plan if things don't go as expected."

This kind of transparency feels risky. You're admitting imperfection. You're acknowledging downsides. Surely that will give ammunition to critics?

In practice, the opposite happens. When you name the trade-offs yourself, you take control of the narrative. Critics were going to identify the downsides anyway. By naming them first, you demonstrate awareness and good faith. You also make it harder for people to argue against straw men.

"You didn't consider the impact on regional teams" is a powerful criticism. "You considered the impact on regional teams but I disagree with your weighting" is a much weaker one.

Justified trade-offs build the credibility that allows you to make difficult decisions. If employees trust that you've genuinely considered the implications, they're more willing to accept outcomes they wouldn't have chosen themselves.

Naming Things Like People

Here's a technique borrowed from organisational culture building: naming practices, programmes, and standards after the people who created or exemplify them.

"The Henderson Protocol" carries different weight than "Standard Operating Procedure 47." "Sarah's Rule" implies history and intention in a way that "Policy Guideline 3.2" does not. "The Mitchell Method" suggests that a real person developed this approach and stands behind it.

Why does this work? Several reasons.

Named things imply heritage. When something is named after a person, there's an implicit story: this person created it, believed in it, and it worked well enough to be formalised. The name carries the weight of that history.

Named things imply accountability. Sarah's Rule has a Sarah. If you have questions about why this rule exists, there's someone, or at least someone's legacy, that can be invoked. Anonymous procedures have no one standing behind them.

Named things are more memorable. "Remember to follow the Henderson Protocol" sticks in the mind better than "Remember to follow SOP 47." The human name creates a cognitive hook.

Named things humanise the organisation. Every named element is a reminder that the organisation was built by people making decisions, not an abstract system generating rules. The name says: a human created this, for human reasons.

This doesn't work for everything. Some things should be anonymous and procedural. Not everything needs the weight of a named tradition. But for important practices, signature approaches, or cultural touchstones, naming creates value.

Consider which of your organisation's practices could be named. Is there a distinctive approach to client service that someone developed? A meeting format that a respected leader introduced? A quality standard that emerged from a specific team's innovation? These are candidates for naming, not as an ego exercise, but as a way of encoding heritage and humanity into organisational practice.

The Warehouse Problem

There's a balance to strike here, and it's important to name explicitly: you can show too much.

I think of this as the warehouse problem. In a well-run retail operation, customers see the shop floor: curated, organised, attractive. They don't see the warehouse: chaotic, utilitarian, full of half-unpacked boxes and inventory management systems. The warehouse is necessary for the shop floor to function, but showing it to customers would create confusion, not transparency.

Organisational decision-making has its own warehouse. The early drafts that were abandoned. The heated debates that were resolved. The political dynamics that shaped what was possible. The failed experiments that informed the successful ones. The uncertainty that existed before the decision crystallised.

Some of this is worth showing: the considered alternatives, the constraints navigated, the trade-offs made. Some of it is not: the internal politics, the dead ends, the moments of genuine confusion.

The distinction isn't about hiding problems or pretending everything was smooth. It's about showing the craft without showing the chaos. People want to know that competent professionals considered the options and made a thoughtful decision. They don't need, or want, a detailed account of every wrong turn and interpersonal dynamic along the way.

Too little transparency: "Here's the new policy." (No indication of thought behind it.)

Right amount: "Here's the new policy. We considered three approaches, and here's why we chose this one. The main trade-off is X, which we're addressing through Y."

Too much transparency: "Here's the new policy. We started with a completely different approach, but then legal raised concerns, and finance pushed back, and there was a lot of disagreement about whether to prioritise speed or thoroughness. At one point we almost went with Option C, but then the sponsor changed and the new person had different priorities..."

The last version doesn't build confidence. It undermines it. It suggests decision-making was more political than principled, more chaotic than considered. Some transparency builds trust; too much erodes it.

The test is: does this information help people understand and accept the decision, or does it create confusion and doubt? If it helps, include it. If it undermines, leave it in the warehouse.

Showing the Makers

One of the simplest ways to showcase craft is to show the people who made something.

Most organisational communications are curiously impersonal. Decisions are attributed to "the company" or "leadership" or "HR." Initiatives are launched without any indication of who developed them. Policies arrive from nowhere, authored by no one.

This anonymity makes organisations feel like machines rather than communities of people. It also misses an opportunity to build connection and credibility.

Consider adding "made by" credits to significant communications:

"This recommendation was developed by a working group including [names], with input from [names]."

"Thank you to [name] and their team for leading this initiative over the past six months."

"The approach we're adopting was originally piloted by [name]'s team in [location]. Thank you for paving the way."

These credits do several things. They give recognition where it's due, which motivates the people involved and signals that contributions are valued. They humanise the decision, making it easier to engage with. They create a contact point: if I have questions, I know who was involved.

For major initiatives, consider more substantial "meet the team" content. Short profiles or interviews with key contributors. A photo of the project team. A brief video where the lead explains the thinking behind the work.

This isn't about ego or self-promotion. It's about making visible the human effort behind organisational outputs. People worked hard on this. They thought carefully. They made difficult judgments. Let's acknowledge that rather than pretending decisions materialise from the corporate ether.

Earning Patience

Here's why all of this matters: showcasing craft earns you patience.

Employees who understand the thought behind decisions are more patient when things aren't perfect. They know trade-offs were considered. They know constraints existed. They trust that problems will be addressed because they've seen evidence of thoughtful management.

Employees who don't see the craft assume the worst. Decisions seem arbitrary. Problems seem like negligence. There's no reservoir of goodwill to draw on when things go wrong, because there's no evidence of competence to justify it.

This patience is particularly valuable during change. Every significant change involves a period of adjustment where things aren't working as well as they will eventually. If employees trust the people leading the change, if they've seen evidence of craft and competence, they'll tolerate this period. If they don't, every problem becomes evidence that the change was a mistake.

Showcasing craft is an investment in future credibility. Every communication that shows the thought behind decisions builds a little more trust. That trust compounds over time. It creates permission to make difficult decisions, take calculated risks, and ask for patience when things are hard.

The invisible organisation, where decisions appear from nowhere and are defended with nothing, earns no such patience. Every problem is met with "I told you so." Every change is resisted because there's no reason to believe it will work. The organisation works against itself.

Show the craft. Show the people. Show the thought. It takes a few extra sentences, a few extra paragraphs, a few extra minutes of explanation. The trust it builds is worth far more.

PART FOUR

MAKING IT WORK

Chapter Twelve: Measuring What Actually Matters

In the early days of digital advertising, marketers became obsessed with a metric called "impressions." An impression was counted every time an ad appeared on someone's screen. The numbers were intoxicating. Millions of impressions! Tens of millions! The campaigns were clearly working. Look at all those impressions!

Except, of course, impressions measured almost nothing useful. An ad that loaded at the bottom of a page no one scrolled to counted as an impression. An ad that appeared for half a second before being scrolled past counted as an impression. An ad that loaded while the user was in another tab, making coffee, counted as an impression.

Impressions measured delivery, not impact. They told you what you'd sent, not what anyone had received, noticed, understood, or acted upon.

Internal communications has its own version of impressions. We call them open rates.

Open rates measure whether someone clicked on an email, which in many email clients happens automatically when the message is previewed. They don't measure whether someone read it, understood it, remembered it, or did anything as a result. They're easy to track, which is why we track them. They're also nearly useless as indicators of actual communication effectiveness.

This chapter is about measuring what matters rather than what's easy. It's about building a measurement framework that tells you whether your communications are actually working, not just whether they're being delivered.

The Measurement Trap

Let me be direct about the state of internal communications measurement: it's mostly theatre.

We produce reports showing open rates, click-through rates, attendance figures, page views. We present these numbers to stakeholders as evidence of impact. We set targets for improving them. We celebrate when they go up and explain away when they go down.

But if you pushed most internal communications professionals, they'd admit these metrics don't really tell them what they need to know. Did employees understand the message? Did it change their behaviour? Did it build or erode trust? Did it make the next communication easier or harder? The dashboard doesn't say.

This creates a peculiar situation. We measure obsessively but learn almost nothing. We have data but not insight. We can tell you exactly how many people opened last week's CEO message (3,847) but not whether anyone could summarise what it said or whether it made them more or less confident in leadership.

The trap is that measuring the wrong things is worse than measuring nothing. When you measure open rates, you optimise for open rates: catchier subject lines, more aggressive send times, more frequent reminders. These tactics might lift your metrics while actively harming your actual effectiveness. More emails with better subject lines create more noise, more fatigue, more cynicism. The numbers go up while the impact goes down.

Breaking out of this trap requires measuring different things. Harder things. Things that actually matter.

The Two Dashboards

The first step toward better measurement is recognising that you need two fundamentally different types of metrics, tracking two fundamentally different things.

The first dashboard is performance metrics. These track the immediate, transactional aspects of communication: did people receive it, engage with it, act on it? Reach, open rates, click-through, attendance, completion rates, response times. These metrics are useful for operational management. They tell you whether your distribution machinery is working. But they're lagging indicators of delivery, not leading indicators of impact.

The second dashboard is brand metrics. These track the underlying health of your communication relationship with employees: do they trust what you say, understand the direction of the organisation, feel connected to its purpose? Trust scores, comprehension measures, advocacy indicators, sentiment trends. These metrics are harder to capture and slower to move, but they're what actually predict organisational resilience.

Most internal communications teams have only the first dashboard. They can tell you everything about delivery and nothing about relationship. This is like a sales team that tracks calls made but not revenue generated, or a marketing team that tracks impressions but not conversions.

The two dashboards serve different purposes and operate on different timescales. Performance metrics should be reviewed frequently: weekly or even daily for active campaigns. Brand metrics should be reviewed quarterly or annually; they don't move fast, and measuring them too often creates noise.

Both matter. Neither alone is sufficient.

Repeat Engagement

If I could add one metric to every internal communications dashboard, it would be repeat engagement: the rate at which employees come back for more.

Repeat engagement measures whether people found value in what you provided. If someone reads your monthly newsletter once and never returns, they're telling you something. If they read it every month and share it with colleagues, they're telling you something else.

This metric is particularly revealing because it's a behavioural indicator, not an attitudinal one. You're not asking people whether they find your communications valuable. You're observing whether they act as if they do. Behaviour doesn't lie.

Tracking repeat engagement requires looking at patterns over time rather than single events. Instead of "how many people opened this email," the question becomes "how many people who opened last month's email also opened this month's?" Instead of "how many people attended the town hall," it's "how many people have attended at least three of the last four town halls?"

The numbers can be sobering. Many organisations discover that a small core of engaged employees accounts for most of their engagement metrics, while a large proportion of the workforce has effectively tuned out. This is valuable information, even when it's uncomfortable.

Repeat engagement also helps you distinguish between curiosity and value. A sensational subject line might generate high opens once, but if people learn that the content doesn't deliver on the promise, they won't come back. Sustainable engagement requires actually providing value, not just capturing attention.

Time to Understanding

Here's a metric almost no one tracks: how long does it take for employees to understand what you're trying to communicate?

Traditional metrics stop at delivery. The message was sent, someone opened it, done. But understanding isn't instant. It develops over time as people encounter information, process it, discuss it with colleagues, and integrate it into their mental model of the organisation.

Time to understanding measures this process. After a major announcement, how long before people can accurately describe what was communicated? How long before misunderstandings are corrected? How long before the message stabilises in the organisation's collective understanding?

Measuring this requires checking comprehension, not just exposure. You might survey a sample of employees a day after an announcement, a week after, and a month after, asking them to explain what was communicated in their own words. The progression tells you how quickly understanding is developing, or not.

You can also track proxies for understanding: the volume and nature of questions received, mentions in internal channels, accuracy of summaries when people discuss the topic. A sudden spike in questions two weeks after an announcement suggests understanding hasn't landed. A decline in mischaracterisations over time suggests it has.

This metric matters because understanding, not delivery, is the actual goal. A communication that's delivered in a day but takes three weeks to understand isn't actually faster than one that's delivered over a week but understood immediately. Time to understanding is what determines when the organisation can act on what's been communicated.

Post-Read Action

The ultimate measure of communication effectiveness is behaviour change. Did the communication result in people doing something different?

This is harder to track than opens and clicks, which is why most teams don't track it. But it's not impossible, and it's infinitely more valuable.

For communications with specific calls to action, post-read action is relatively straightforward. You communicated about a new process: did people adopt it? You announced a training programme: did people enrol? You asked teams to update their information: did they?

The tracking requires connecting communication data with behavioural data. Who received the message about the new process? Of those, who has used the new process? What's the gap, and what does it tell you?

For communications without specific calls to action, broader messages about strategy, values, or organisational direction, post-read action is fuzzier but still trackable. You might look at leading indicators: did the communication prompt conversations, questions, or mentions in other contexts? Did it shift sentiment in subsequent surveys? Did it provide language that people now use when discussing the topic?

The key insight is that communication without behaviour change is just noise. If your strategic update doesn't change how people think about their work, it hasn't worked, regardless of how many people opened it.

The Trust Pulse

Brand metrics require periodic measurement through surveys or other feedback mechanisms. The most important of these is what I call the trust pulse: a regular check on the underlying health of the communication relationship.

The trust pulse should be simple: a handful of questions asked consistently over time. Complexity adds noise without adding insight. What you want is a reliable signal that tells you whether things are getting better or worse.

Core questions might include:

"I trust the information I receive from leadership." **(Trust)**

"I understand the organisation's direction and priorities." **(Comprehension)**

"Communications from the organisation are relevant to my work." **(Relevance)**

"When something important happens, I hear about it through official channels before I hear about it through rumour." **(Timeliness)**

"I would recommend how this organisation communicates as an example for others to follow." **(Advocacy)**

Each question targets a different dimension of communication effectiveness. Together, they provide a reasonably complete picture of the relationship.

Consistency matters more than comprehensiveness. Ask the same questions the same way every time. This lets you track trends and identify shifts. Adding, changing, or removing questions breaks the comparison and reduces the value of the data.

Frequency should balance signal and noise. Quarterly is often right for larger organisations: frequent enough to catch trends, infrequent enough that each measurement is meaningful. Some organisations pulse monthly during periods of significant change, then reduce to quarterly once things stabilise.

Measuring Understanding, Not Satisfaction

Many organisations survey employees about communications, but they ask the wrong questions. "Are you satisfied with internal communications?" tells you whether people are happy but not whether they understand.

Satisfaction and understanding are different things. Someone can be satisfied with communications they don't understand, perhaps they're just glad the emails are short. Someone can be dissatisfied with communications they understand perfectly well, perhaps they understand that the news is bad.

Understanding questions test comprehension, not feelings:

"In your own words, what are the organisation's top three priorities this year?"

"What is the main reason behind the recent change to [specific initiative]?"

"What should you do differently as a result of [specific communication]?"

These questions have right and wrong answers, or at least better and worse answers. You can evaluate responses for accuracy, completeness, and alignment with what was intended. The gap between what was communicated and what was understood is the gap you're trying to close.

This kind of measurement is more labour-intensive than satisfaction surveys. You can't just count responses; you have to read and evaluate them. But the insight is proportionally more valuable. Knowing that 67% of employees are "satisfied" with communications tells you almost nothing. Knowing that only 34% can accurately describe the organisation's strategic priorities tells you something actionable.

The Internal NPS

The Net Promoter Score, asking customers how likely they are to recommend a product or service, has become ubiquitous in customer experience measurement. The same approach can work for internal communications.

The internal NPS asks: "How likely are you to recommend how this organisation communicates to someone considering a job here?" or, for specific programmes, "How likely are you to recommend this programme to a colleague?"

Like the customer NPS, this produces a score from -100 to +100 based on the balance of promoters (9-10 ratings) to detractors (0-6 ratings). The score itself is useful, but more useful is tracking how it changes over time and how it compares across different programmes, channels, or topics.

The power of the NPS question is that it forces an overall evaluation. Someone might have mixed feelings about a programme, some good aspects, some bad, but the recommendation question forces them to net it out. Would they put their own reputation behind this by recommending it? That's a higher bar than satisfaction.

You can also ask the follow-up: "What's the primary reason for your score?" This generates qualitative data about what's working and what isn't, in employees' own words.

Building the Dashboard

Let me pull this together into a practical framework for a dual-dashboard measurement system.

The performance dashboard tracks delivery and engagement:

Reach: what percentage of the target audience received the communication?

Engagement: what percentage engaged with it (opened, clicked, attended, etc.)?

Action: what percentage completed the intended action, if applicable?

Support volume: how many questions or issues were raised?

Response time: how quickly were questions answered?

This dashboard updates frequently: weekly for ongoing programmes, in real-time for major campaigns. It answers the question: is our distribution machinery working?

The brand dashboard tracks relationship and understanding:

Trust pulse: composite score from regular survey questions.

Comprehension: percentage who can accurately describe key messages when tested.

Repeat engagement: percentage who engage with multiple communications over time.

Advocacy: internal NPS or equivalent recommendation metric.

Sentiment trend: directional indicator of how feeling about communications is shifting.

This dashboard updates quarterly. It answers the question: is our communication relationship healthy?

Neither dashboard alone is sufficient. Performance metrics without brand metrics leads to optimising engagement while eroding trust. Brand metrics without performance metrics means you can't diagnose operational problems. Both together give you a complete picture.

What Gets Measured Gets Managed

I want to close with a word of caution. Measurement shapes behaviour, not just the behaviour of communication teams, but the behaviour of everyone who knows what's being measured.

If you measure open rates, you'll optimise for open rates. That might mean more sensational subject lines, more frequent sends, more aggressive targeting. The metric improves while the experience degrades.

If you measure understanding, you'll optimise for understanding. That might mean clearer writing, better structure, more follow-up, more support. The metric improves and so does the experience.

Choose your metrics carefully, because they'll determine what you become. The metrics in this chapter, repeat engagement, time to understanding, post-read action, trust pulse, are harder to track than opens and clicks. They require more effort, more nuance, more judgment.

But they measure what actually matters. And in the long run, measuring what matters is the only way to create what matters.

Chapter Thirteen: The Operating System

Guardrails, Tiers, and Style Guides

Everything we've discussed so far, leading with meaning, telling stories, managing uncertainty, designing moments, supporting at the point of need, requires something to work at scale: systems.

Not bureaucracy. Not endless approval chains and rigid templates that drain creativity and slow everything down. Systems. The operational infrastructure that turns good intentions into consistent practice, that ensures quality doesn't depend on who happens to be working on a particular communication, that makes the right approach the easy approach.

Most internal communications teams operate on talent and effort. When there's a skilled person with enough time, the work is good. When there isn't, it isn't. This is exhausting and unsustainable. It means quality varies wildly. It means institutional knowledge walks out the door when people leave. It means every communication is reinvented from scratch.

This chapter is about building the operating system that makes excellence the default rather than the exception. It's deliberately practical: frameworks, criteria, templates that can be implemented without requiring approval from seventeen stakeholders or a six-month transformation programme.

The Tiering Model

The first operational question for any communication is: what level of investment does this warrant? Not every message deserves the same treatment. A reminder about car park maintenance shouldn't receive the same production value as the CEO's strategic update. But without clear criteria, these decisions are made ad hoc, inconsistently, based on whoever shouts loudest or happens to be in the room.

A tiering model creates explicit criteria for matching investment to importance.

Tier One communications are your most significant: announcements that affect the entire organisation, major strategic shifts, leadership changes, crisis responses, annual milestones. These warrant premium treatment: dedicated channels, high production value, leadership involvement, robust support infrastructure, designed moments rather than simple messages. Tier One communications should be rare. If everything is Tier One, nothing is.

Tier Two communications are significant but not exceptional: programme launches, policy changes, quarterly updates, departmental news that affects multiple teams. These warrant good treatment: thoughtful writing, appropriate formatting, clear support pathways, but not the full premium package. Tier Two is your workhorse category, where most substantive communications live.

Tier Three communications are routine: process reminders, administrative updates, regular cadence communications, narrowly relevant information. These should be efficient and clear. No elaborate production, no extensive narrative, just well-organised information delivered appropriately. Tier Three communications shouldn't try to be more than they are. Dressing up routine information wastes resources and dilutes the impact of genuinely significant messages.

The criteria for tiering should be explicit. You might consider:

Scope: how many people are affected? Organisation-wide communications tier higher than departmental ones.

Impact: how significant is the effect on people's work or lives? Changes to compensation tier higher than changes to meeting room booking.

Sensitivity: how emotionally charged is the topic? Reorganisations tier higher than system upgrades.

Strategic importance: how central is this to organisational priorities? Strategic initiatives tier higher than operational improvements.

Novelty: how unexpected or unprecedented is this? First-time communications tier higher than recurring ones.

Different organisations will weight these factors differently. The important thing is having criteria that everyone understands and applies consistently.

The tiering decision should happen early, before you start drafting, before you book the town hall slot, before you engage designers. It shapes everything that follows. A Tier One communication needs time for proper production. A Tier Three communication shouldn't be waiting for production that it doesn't need.

Broadcast, Narrowcast, and Channel Selection

Closely related to tiering is the question of channel selection. Should this be a broadcast to everyone, a narrowcast to specific audiences, or something in between?

The default in most organisations is to broadcast too much. When in doubt, send it to everyone. This feels safe, nobody can complain they weren't informed, but it creates noise that drowns out genuinely important communications.

A better approach is to default to the narrowest appropriate audience:

Who actually needs this information? Not who might be interested, not who might want to know, but who genuinely needs it to do their work or understand their situation.

Who would be harmed by not receiving it? This is a different question. Some information isn't strictly necessary but its absence would create problems: people would feel excluded, rumours would fill the void, trust would be damaged.

The appropriate audience is the union of these two groups. Everyone who needs the information, plus everyone who would be harmed by not receiving it. Often, this is significantly smaller than "everyone."

Channel selection follows similar logic:

Live channels (town halls, webinars, meetings) are appropriate when: interaction is valuable, questions are expected, emotional resonance matters, the topic is complex enough to benefit from discussion.

Asynchronous channels (email, intranet, video) are appropriate when: people need to access information at different times, the message needs to be referenced later, the topic is straightforward enough not to require discussion.

Written channels are appropriate when: precision matters, people need to search or reference, translation is required, legal documentation is important.

Visual or video channels are appropriate when: emotional connection matters, demonstration is valuable, personal presence from leaders adds credibility.

Most significant communications benefit from a multi-channel approach: a live session for those who can attend, a recording for those who can't, a written summary for reference, a support channel for questions. The channels complement rather than duplicate each other.

The Style Guide

Every internal communications function should have a style guide. Not a hundred-page brand manual that nobody reads, but a practical reference that answers the questions communicators actually face.

The style guide should cover:

Voice and tone. How do we sound? What's our personality as an organisation? This isn't about rigid rules; tone should flex based on context. It's about establishing a recognisable identity. Are we formal or conversational? Serious or warm? Direct or diplomatic? The guide should provide examples of each tone and guidance on when each is appropriate.

Language standards. What words do we use and avoid? This includes jargon to eliminate, plain-language alternatives for corporate speak, and terminology that's specific to your organisation. It should also cover inclusive language guidelines: how to write about people with disabilities, gender-neutral language, avoiding assumptions about family structures.

Privacy-safe personalisation. We covered this in Chapter Eight, but the style guide should codify it. What data can be referenced in communications? What phrasing is appropriate for light-touch personalisation? What crosses the line into creepy?

Cultural localisation. For global organisations, what needs to adapt for different markets? This might include formality levels, humour, references and examples, and sensitivity to local contexts. The guide should identify what must be localised versus what can remain global.

Accessibility standards. How do we ensure communications work for everyone? This includes plain language principles, formatting for screen readers, captioning requirements for video, colour contrast for visual materials.

Format standards. What do our templates look like? What's the structure for different communication types? This creates consistency and saves time. Communicators aren't reinventing basic formatting for every message.

The style guide should be a living document, updated as you learn and as the organisation evolves. It should be easily accessible, ideally integrated into the tools people use to create communications. A style guide that lives in a forgotten SharePoint folder helps no one.

The Service Level Agreement

In Chapter Nine, we discussed the importance of support at the point of need. The operational mechanism for ensuring this happens consistently is a service level agreement: an explicit commitment to what support you'll provide and how responsive you'll be.

A communications service level might specify:

Response time commitments. Questions acknowledged within four hours during business hours. Substantive response within one business day. Complex questions requiring escalation within three business days. These times should be realistic but ambitious: achievable with effort, not so generous that they permit neglect.

Channel availability. Which channels are available for questions (email, Slack, phone, office hours)? When are they staffed? What's the expected response time for each?

Escalation paths. When a question exceeds the front-line team's authority or knowledge, what happens? Who escalates to whom? What's the expected timeline for escalated questions?

Coverage for major communications. For Tier One communications, what additional support is provided? Named back-stops, extended hours, additional channels?

Feedback loops. How is question data collected, analysed, and used to improve future communications?

The service level should be published, both to set expectations with employees and to create accountability within the team. If you've committed to four-hour acknowledgment, you'd better have the capacity to deliver it.

Some organisations tie service levels to communication tiers. Tier One communications receive enhanced support: dedicated channels, named contacts, extended hours. Tier Three communications receive standard support: a general inbox with standard response times. This ensures resources are concentrated where they matter most.

Decision Trees and Playbooks

For recurring decisions, document the criteria in a decision tree or playbook. This captures institutional knowledge and ensures consistency even when experienced team members aren't available.

A channel selection decision tree might start with: "Does this require interaction?" If yes, consider live channels. If no, proceed to: "Does this need to be referenced later?" If yes, include written materials. And so on.

A crisis communications playbook might specify: who needs to be notified, in what order, through what channels, within what timeframe. What approvals are required? What templates are available? What support infrastructure needs to be activated?

An event communications playbook might cover: when to start promoting, what channels to use at each stage, what follow-up is required afterward.

These playbooks don't eliminate judgment. Communications always requires judgment. But they ensure that routine decisions don't require reinventing the wheel every time. They also make it possible for less experienced team members to handle more situations confidently.

Using Disruption as a Window

Here's an operational principle that might seem counterintuitive: periods of organisational disruption are the best times to change how you communicate.

When things are stable, people resist change. "Why are we doing this differently? The old way worked fine." The activation energy required to shift behaviour is high.

When things are already disrupted, a reorganisation, a leadership transition, a crisis, a major transformation, that resistance drops. People expect things to be different. They're already adapting to change. Adding one more change to the pile is easier than introducing change when everything else is stable.

This creates a window for innovation. Want to introduce a new communication format? Do it during a period of broader change. Want to shift from email-heavy to channel-based communication? Launch it alongside a reorganisation when information flows are being rebuilt anyway. Want to pilot video updates from leadership? Try it during a crisis when people are hungry for direct communication.

The disruption provides cover. If the new approach doesn't work perfectly, there's a ready explanation: "we're all adjusting to a lot of changes." If it does work, you've established a new norm that persists after the disruption passes.

This isn't about being opportunistic during difficult times. It's about recognising that change is easier when the system is already in motion. A rolling stone is easier to redirect than a stationary one.

Making It Stick

Operational systems only work if people actually use them. The best tiering model in the world is useless if communicators ignore it. The most thoughtful style guide accomplishes nothing if it sits unread.

Making systems stick requires several things.

Simplicity. If the system is too complex, people will work around it. A tiering model with fifteen levels won't be used. Three levels, Tier One, Tier Two, Tier Three, is memorable and practical.

Integration. Build the systems into existing workflows rather than adding extra steps. If tiering decisions happen in the briefing template people already use, they'll happen. If they require a separate form, they won't.

Accountability. Someone should be responsible for ensuring systems are followed. Not as a compliance exercise, but as a quality standard. Regular reviews of recent communications: did we tier appropriately? Did we follow the style guide? Did we meet our service levels?

Evolution. Systems should improve based on experience. What's working? What's creating unnecessary friction? What edge cases aren't covered? Regular retrospectives keep systems relevant and useful.

The goal isn't perfection. It's consistency and improvement over time. Good systems make good practice easier and more reliable. They free up mental energy for the creative and strategic work that can't be systematised. They ensure that quality doesn't depend on luck.

Strategy without systems is just aspiration. Systems are how aspiration becomes reality.

Chapter Fourteen: Getting Started

The First 90 Days

You've read twelve chapters of principles, frameworks, and techniques. You're possibly feeling one of two things: energised by the possibilities, or overwhelmed by the gap between where you are and where you could be.

Both reactions are reasonable. The principles in this book represent a significant shift from how most organisations approach internal communications. Implementing all of them would be a multi-year transformation. Nobody has the bandwidth for that, least of all internal communications teams who are already stretched thin keeping the daily machinery running.

So let's be practical. This chapter is about starting, not about transforming everything at once, but about building momentum through focused action. The first 90 days. Quick wins that demonstrate value. A roadmap that's ambitious enough to matter and realistic enough to achieve.

Transformation is a big word. Let's start with progress.

The Quick Wins

Before we get to strategy and roadmaps, let's identify five things you can implement in the first month with minimal approval, minimal budget, and minimal disruption. These aren't the most important changes. They're the most achievable ones. Their purpose is to create early momentum and demonstrate that a different approach is possible.

Quick win one: rewrite your next opening paragraph. Take whatever significant communication is next in your queue and rewrite the opening paragraph to lead with meaning. Don't bury the "so what." Put it first. Before you explain what's happening, explain why it matters. This costs nothing, requires no approval, and you'll likely see immediate improvement in engagement and comprehension. Do this for every communication for the next month and observe the difference.

Quick win two: add a "You're here" module. For any ongoing programme or change initiative, create a simple status indicator: "You're here. Next up..." Add it to every communication about that programme. This takes fifteen minutes to create and transforms how people experience the change, from uncertain waiting to visible progress.

Quick win three: put a human back-stop on your next Tier One communication. Before you send the next significant announcement, identify a named person who will own questions and support. Put their name, email, and phone number prominently in the communication. Commit to a response time. This doesn't require new resources. Someone is already answering questions; you're just making them visible and accountable.

Quick win four: kill one recurring communication. Every organisation has communications that continue out of inertia rather than value. The weekly update nobody reads. The monthly report that duplicates information available elsewhere. The newsletter that's been running since 2007 and hasn't been evaluated since. Find one and stop it. If nobody notices, you've freed up capacity. If people complain, you've learned something valuable about what they actually want.

Quick win five: tell one story. In your next all-hands, town hall, or significant communication, include one genuine story. A customer impact. An employee who exemplified values. A challenge overcome. Not a case study, but a story with narrative arc, human characters, and emotional resonance. See how people respond.

These five actions don't require a transformation programme. They require decisions you can make this week. Start there.

The Quick-Start Diagnostic

Before you can improve, you need to know where you stand. The following diagnostic covers the key principles from this book. For each question, assess your current state honestly, not where you'd like to be, but where you actually are.

Leading with meaning: Do your communications consistently explain why before what? Would employees say your messages help them understand significance, or just inform them of facts?

Storytelling: Do you regularly include human narratives in your communications? Could employees recall a story from your last major announcement?

Managing uncertainty: For ongoing changes, can employees see where things stand and what happens next? Do you have predictable communication cadences that people can rely on?

Friction and ritual: Have you audited your communications for unnecessary friction? Do you have intentional rituals that mark significant moments?

Designed moments: Do your most important communications feel different from routine ones? Is there visible investment that signals significance?

Personalisation: Do you tailor communications appropriately without crossing into surveillance? Can employees choose what they receive?

Support infrastructure: Is it easy for employees to get questions answered? Do you have clear ownership and response time commitments?

Pilots and proof: Do you build belief through well-run pilots before scaling? Do you capture and deploy stories from early adopters?

Showcasing craft: Do employees see the thought and effort behind decisions? Do they understand the trade-offs that were made?

Measurement: Do you track understanding and behaviour change, not just opens and clicks? Do you have brand metrics alongside performance metrics?

Operating systems: Do you have clear tiering criteria, style guides, and service levels? Are these documented and consistently applied?

For each area, rate yourself: strong, adequate, or needs work. The areas marked "needs work" are your priorities. The areas marked "strong" are your foundations to build from.

Building the Case

Unless you're the sole decision-maker, and even then, you'll need to bring others along. Leadership, stakeholders, your own team. Here's how to make the case for a different approach.

Start with the problem, not the solution. Don't lead with "we should tell more stories" or "we need to invest in designed moments." Lead with the gap: "Our communications aren't landing. Employees can't describe our strategic priorities. Change programmes are meeting resistance that better communication could address. We're working harder but not achieving more."

Use their language. If leadership cares about employee engagement scores, connect communication quality to engagement. If they care about change programme success rates, show how communication approach affects adoption. If they care about efficiency, demonstrate how investing in support reduces the time spent managing confusion and resistance.

Propose experiments, not transformations. "I'd like to completely overhaul our communications approach" is a big ask that triggers big concerns. "I'd like to pilot a different approach for our next major announcement and measure the results" is much easier to approve. Start small, prove value, expand.

Show, don't tell. Rather than explaining what better communications could look like, demonstrate it. Rewrite an existing communication using the principles in this book. Put the original and the revision side by side. The difference will be obvious, and more persuasive than any argument.

Find allies. Who else in the organisation cares about this? HR leaders frustrated by change resistance. Programme managers struggling with adoption. Executives who feel their messages aren't getting through. These are your allies. Build a coalition of people who share the problem, even if they haven't articulated the solution.

Accept incremental progress. You probably won't get everything you want immediately. That's fine. Get something. A pilot. A budget for one initiative. Permission to try a different approach for one communication. Incremental progress beats ambitious stagnation.

The Pilot Plan

Chapter Ten covered pilots in depth, but let's apply that specifically to piloting a new communications approach.

Select a suitable initiative. You want something significant enough to matter but contained enough to manage. A programme launch, a policy change, a system implementation. Ideally, something where the current approach would be "send an email and hope for the best." The contrast with a designed approach will be stark.

Define what "different" means. Based on your diagnostic, what specifically will you do differently? Perhaps: lead with meaning in all communications, create a change map with visible status, establish a named back-stop with published response times, design a launch moment rather than just sending an announcement, capture stories from early adopters. Be specific about what you're testing.

Resource it properly. This is crucial. A pilot that fails because of inadequate resources proves nothing except that under-resourced initiatives fail. Concentrate support on the pilot. Make it impossible to fail for reasons of neglect. You want to test the approach, not the resourcing.

Measure appropriately. Define success criteria before you start. What will you measure? Understanding (can people explain what was communicated)? Engagement (do people come to sessions, ask questions, participate)? Adoption (do people actually change behaviour)? Sentiment (do people feel well-informed and supported)? Compare to similar previous initiatives where possible.

Document everything. Capture what you did, how it went, what you learned. Testimonials from participants. Before-and-after comparisons. Quantitative metrics where available. This documentation becomes your evidence base for expanding the approach.

Tell the story. When the pilot succeeds, and if you've done it right, it will, tell the story. Share results with leadership. Highlight what was different and why it worked. Use the pilot as proof that a different approach delivers different outcomes.

The 90-Day Roadmap

Here's a sequenced plan for the first three months.

Days 1-30: Foundation. Implement the five quick wins. Complete the diagnostic. Identify your priority areas. Select a pilot initiative. Build your coalition of allies. Begin documenting your current state, metrics, feedback, examples, so you have a baseline to compare against.

Days 31-60: Pilot. Launch your pilot initiative using the principles from this book. Resource it heavily. Document as you go. Gather feedback continuously. Adjust based on what you learn. Start capturing stories and testimonials from participants.

Days 61-90: Learn and expand. Evaluate pilot results against your success criteria. Document lessons learned. Share results with stakeholders. Make the case for expanding the approach. Identify the next initiative to apply the principles to. Begin building the operational infrastructure, tiering criteria, style guide elements, service level commitments, that will make the approach sustainable.

By day 90, you should have: demonstrated proof that a different approach works, built credibility with stakeholders, identified what needs to adapt for your specific context, and established momentum for continued progress.

This isn't transformation. It's the foundation for transformation. The work continues well beyond 90 days. But you'll have moved from theory to practice, from aspiration to evidence.

What You're Not Trying to Do

A word on scope. In 90 days, you're not trying to:

Overhaul all communications. You're piloting a different approach with one initiative, not transforming everything simultaneously.

Build perfect systems. You're establishing initial frameworks that will evolve, not creating permanent infrastructure.

Convert all sceptics. You're building evidence and allies, not winning every argument.

Achieve final metrics. You're establishing baselines and demonstrating direction, not hitting ultimate targets.

The 90-day goal is momentum, not completion. Prove the approach works. Build credibility. Create the conditions for continued progress. That's enough.

Sustaining Progress

The risk with any improvement effort is that initial energy fades and old habits return. Here's how to sustain progress beyond the first 90 days.

Make it visible. Share results regularly. Celebrate successes. Keep the new approach on leadership's radar. Visibility creates accountability and attracts support.

Build it into workflows. The more the new approach is embedded in how work gets done, templates, checklists, review processes, the more it persists. Make the right way the easy way.

Develop capability. Train your team on the principles. Create resources they can reference. Build skill, not just compliance.

Measure continuously. Keep tracking the metrics that matter. Show progress over time. Use data to identify where further improvement is needed.

Expand deliberately. Each successful initiative creates permission for the next one. Each story of success builds the case for wider adoption. Expand at a pace that maintains quality.

The principles in this book aren't a one-time fix. They're a different way of thinking about internal communications, one that requires ongoing attention and continuous improvement. The 90-day plan gets you started. What happens after determines whether it lasts.

Conclusion

The Journey, Not Just the Train

We started this book with an uncomfortable truth: most internal communications go unread, misunderstood, or forgotten within hours. We end it with a different truth, one that I hope feels more like possibility than burden: it doesn't have to be this way.

The principles in these pages aren't complicated. Lead with meaning. Tell stories. Manage uncertainty. Design moments. Support at the point of need. Show the craft. Measure what matters. None of this requires genius-level insight or revolutionary technology. It requires a shift in perspective, from communications as logistics to communications as experience.

For decades, internal communications has optimised for the wrong things. We've made the train faster. More channels, more frequency, more sophisticated distribution, more granular targeting. We've built impressive machinery for getting information from Point A to Point B.

What we haven't done is make the journey better.

The train is a means, not an end. Nobody wants to receive communications. They want to understand what's happening, feel connected to the organisation's purpose, trust that someone competent is in charge, know that they matter. These are human needs, and they're not satisfied by faster trains.

Making the journey better means asking different questions. Not "how do we reach more people?" but "how do we create more meaning?" Not "how do we increase open rates?" but "how do we build trust?" Not "how do we communicate more efficiently?" but "how do we communicate more effectively?"

The answers to these questions are what this book has been about.

Psychological Value Is Real Value

One of the core arguments running through these chapters is that psychological value, how things feel, not just what they are, is real value. It's not soft. It's not secondary. It's the primary determinant of whether your communications achieve anything at all.

The Uber map doesn't make the car arrive faster. The "just add an egg" recipe isn't meaningfully harder. The Gmail invite doesn't make the product better. But each of these creates value, real, measurable, consequential value, through psychology rather than function.

Internal communications has been slow to embrace this reality. There's a lingering sense that focusing on how things feel is somehow less serious than focusing on what things are. That experience design is a nice-to-have, while information delivery is the real work.

This is backwards. The information is table stakes. Everyone can deliver information. What separates effective communications from ineffective ones is whether that information creates understanding, builds trust, and enables action. Those outcomes are determined by psychology, by how communications are framed, packaged, delivered, and supported.

Creating psychological value isn't manipulation. It's respect. It's acknowledging that employees are human beings who experience communications, not data pipes who simply receive them. It's taking seriously the reality that perception shapes behaviour, that meaning drives action, that trust determines outcomes.

The organisations that understand this have an enormous advantage. They can navigate change more smoothly because employees trust leadership's competence and intentions. They can weather crises because there's a reservoir of goodwill to draw on. They can ask for difficult things because they've built the credibility to ask.

This advantage isn't built through any single communication. It's built through sustained investment in meaning, trust, and experience. It's the compound interest of taking employees seriously, communication after communication, year after year.

The Counterintuitive Approach

Several times throughout this book, I've advocated for approaches that might seem counterintuitive.

Start with a small pilot instead of a broad launch, even though it seems slower.

Add friction through rituals, even though we usually try to remove friction.

Show the trade-offs and constraints behind decisions, even though that reveals imperfection.

Invest heavily in support after sending, even though the sending feels like the main event.

Limit access to create scarcity, even though reach is usually the goal.

These approaches work because they're grounded in how humans actually process information and make decisions, rather than how we imagine they should. They acknowledge the reality of attention scarcity, trust dynamics, and meaning-making that shapes whether communications land.

The conventional approaches, broadcast everything, hide the sausage-making, optimise for delivery metrics, treat communications as transactions, aren't wrong because they're malicious. They're wrong because they're based on a model of humans as rational information processors, which we're not.

When you design for how people actually work rather than how you wish they worked, counterintuitive approaches become obviously correct. Of course a visible pilot builds more belief than an invisible broad launch. People trust what they can see. Of course a ritual creates more meaning than a notification. Humans are ceremony-making creatures. Of course showing trade-offs builds more trust than pretending everything is perfect. We know decisions involve trade-offs.

The counterintuitive becomes intuitive once you shift your model.

What's At Stake

I've tried throughout this book to be practical rather than preachy. Frameworks, templates, checklists, tools you can use tomorrow. But let me, just for a moment in these closing pages, speak to what's actually at stake.

Internal communications isn't a support function. It's the nervous system of the organisation. It's how strategy becomes action, how values become behaviour, how leadership intent becomes frontline reality. When it works, it's invisible. Things just happen. When it fails, nothing else can fully succeed.

Poor internal communications makes change harder. Every initiative faces more resistance than it should. Every announcement breeds more confusion than clarity. Every transformation takes longer and costs more because the organisation can't align around what's happening and why.

Poor internal communications erodes culture. When employees don't understand the organisation's direction, don't trust its leadership, don't feel connected to its purpose, that's not just an engagement problem. It's an existential problem. Culture becomes fragmented, cynical, self-protective. The organisation stops functioning as one thing and starts functioning as many competing things.

Poor internal communications wastes human potential. Employees who don't understand what they're working toward, who don't see how their contribution matters, who feel like interchangeable units rather than valued humans, these employees don't bring their full selves to work. The organisation gets compliance instead of commitment, presence instead of engagement.

This is what's at stake. Not open rates. Not communication metrics. The organisation's ability to function, to change, to engage its people in shared purpose. That's what effective internal communications enables. That's what ineffective internal communications undermines.

The Only Thing Left

The principles are here. The frameworks are here. The examples, the templates, the diagnostic tools, the roadmaps.

The only thing left is to start.

Not to transform everything. Not to implement every principle simultaneously. Not to wait until conditions are perfect or resources are abundant or leadership is fully aligned.

Just to start. One communication that leads with meaning. One story told well. One change map that makes progress visible. One pilot run properly. One measurement that tracks understanding rather than opens.

Small actions, consistently applied, compound over time. The organisation that's marginally better at communications this month becomes noticeably better next quarter becomes significantly better next year. The gap between organisations that invest in this and organisations that don't widens with every communication cycle.

You don't need permission to start. The first quick wins require no approval, no budget, no transformation programme. They require only a decision to do the next communication differently.

The trains will keep running. The machinery of organisational communication will continue to operate. Messages will be sent, channels will be monitored, metrics will be tracked.

The question is whether that machinery serves human needs, understanding, trust, meaning, connection, or merely moves information from place to place.

Make the journey better. Start today.

Appendices

Appendix A: Templates And Checklists

The Quick-Start Diagnostic

Use this diagnostic to assess your current state across the key principles. For each area, mark your honest assessment: Strong (S), Adequate (A), or Needs Work (N). Areas marked "Needs Work" are your priorities.

Leading with Meaning

☐ Do communications explain "why" before "what"?

☐ Can employees articulate the significance of recent announcements?

☐ Is the opening paragraph of major communications focused on meaning?

☐ Do you apply the "so what?" test before sending?

Storytelling

☐ Do major communications include human narratives?

☐ Is there a customer story in every all-hands meeting?

☐ Do you have a system for collecting and cataloguing stories?

☐ Can employees recall stories from recent communications?

Managing Uncertainty

☐ For ongoing changes, can employees see current status?

- [ ] Do you provide "what happens next" information?
- [ ] Is there a predictable cadence for updates?
- [ ] Do you reframe waiting periods as preparation time?

Friction and Ritual

- [ ] Have you audited communications for unnecessary blockers?
- [ ] Are significant moments marked with intentional rituals?
- [ ] Do you invite small co-creation steps ("just add an egg")?
- [ ] Are there closure ceremonies when initiatives complete?

Designed Moments

- [ ] Do Tier One communications feel different from routine ones?
- [ ] Is leadership time visibly invested in significant announcements?
- [ ] Do you create artifacts that extend beyond the initial communication?
- [ ] Is there an "unboxing experience" for major news?

Personalisation

- [ ] Do you tailor communications without crossing into surveillance?
- [ ] Can employees choose what they receive (opt-in)?
- [ ] Do you use light-touch phrasing rather than data playback?
- [ ] Are milestone celebrations genuinely personal?

Support Infrastructure

- [ ] Is there a named human behind every major communication?
- [ ] Are contact details prominent (not hidden)?
- [ ] Do you have published response time commitments?

☐ Is support available through multiple channels?

Pilots and Social Proof

☐ Do you run well-resourced pilots before broad rollouts?

☐ Do you select pilot participants strategically for influence?

☐ Are before-and-after stories captured and deployed?

☐ Is scarcity used to create desire rather than mandates to create compliance?

Showcasing Craft

☐ Do employees see the thought behind decisions?

☐ Are trade-offs explained rather than hidden?

☐ Do you show the people involved in creating initiatives?

☐ Is there "how it's made" content for significant programmes?

Measurement

☐ Do you track understanding, not just opens?

☐ Do you measure repeat engagement?

☐ Is there a trust pulse alongside performance metrics?

☐ Do insights from measurement inform future communications?

Operating Systems

☐ Do you have clear tiering criteria?

☐ Is there a documented style guide?

☐ Are service levels defined and published?

☐ Are decision trees available for recurring choices?

Scoring: Count your responses. More than 10 "Needs Work" responses suggests significant opportunity for improvement. Focus first on areas where multiple items are marked "N". These represent systemic gaps rather than isolated issues.

Tier One Announcement Template

Use this template for your most significant communications: major strategic shifts, leadership changes, reorganisations, crisis responses, annual milestones.

Pre-Communication Checklist

☐ Tiering confirmed: this genuinely warrants Tier One treatment

☐ Key message defined: one sentence capturing the meaning

☐ Narrative arc prepared: origin, struggle, breakthrough, impact

☐ Trade-offs identified: what we're acknowledging openly

☐ Support infrastructure ready: named owner, channels, response times

☐ Artifacts designed: summary document, visual element, or physical item

☐ Delivery format confirmed: live component, recorded element, written summary

☐ Questions anticipated: FAQ prepared, back-stop briefed

Communication Structure

Opening (meaning first): Two to three sentences establishing why this matters. Answer the "so what?" before explaining the "what." Lead with significance, not facts.

Context: Brief background that positions this announcement. How does it connect to what people already know? What's the situation that gave rise to this?

The narrative: The story of this change using the story spine. Where did this come from? What challenge or opportunity are we addressing? What did we figure out or decide? What changes as a result?

What it means for employees: Specific implications for the audience. What's different for them? What stays the same? What should they expect?

The trade-offs (if applicable): What we considered, what we chose, and why. What downsides are we accepting and how are we addressing them?

What happens next: Clear timeline with milestones. "You're here. Next up..." Include dates where possible.

Support information: Named contact, multiple channels, response time commitment. Prominent placement, not buried in a footer.

Close: Human sign-off. Personal commitment from a leader. Invitation to engage.

Post-Communication Checklist

☐ Support channels active and staffed

☐ Back-stop monitoring for questions

☐ Question tracking in place

☐ Follow-up communication scheduled

☐ Feedback mechanisms ready

☐ Success metrics defined

Change Map Template

Use this template to create visibility into any significant change or programme.

Programme Overview: Programme name, one-sentence description, programme owner (named person), start date, expected completion.

Current Phase: Phase name, phase description (one to two sentences), phase start date, expected phase completion.

Key Activities This Phase: List three to five key activities underway.

You Are Here: Visual representation showing completed phases, current phase (highlighted), upcoming phases. Simple format: boxes or circles connected by lines, with clear indication of current position.

What's Next: Next milestone, expected date, what it means for you. Following milestone, expected date.

Key Dates Coming Up: List three to five upcoming dates with associated events or milestones.

How to Get Help: Questions and support (named person, email, phone, Slack), office hours (day, time, location/link), FAQ and resources (link), urgent issues (contact method).

Update Cadence: "This change map is updated every [frequency]. Next update: [date]." Last updated: [date].

Friction Audit Checklist

Use this checklist to identify unnecessary friction in your communications.

Access Friction

☐ Can people find the communication easily?

☐ Does it work on mobile devices?

☐ Is it accessible to people using screen readers?

☐ Does it load quickly?

☐ Is it available in necessary languages?

Comprehension Friction

☐ Is jargon explained or eliminated?

☐ Are acronyms spelled out on first use?

☐ Is the reading level appropriate for the audience?

☐ Are key points easy to identify?

☐ Is necessary context provided?

Navigation Friction

☐ Can people find the specific information they need?

- ☐ Is the structure logical and scannable?
- ☐ Are links clearly labelled and functional?
- ☐ Is the most important information prominent?
- ☐ Can people return to this communication later and find what they need?

Action Friction

- ☐ Is the required action clear?
- ☐ Is the deadline unambiguous?
- ☐ Are the steps to complete the action obvious?
- ☐ Are there unnecessary steps that could be eliminated?
- ☐ Do links go directly to where people need to go?

Support Friction

- ☐ Is it clear who to contact with questions?
- ☐ Is contact information prominent (not buried)?
- ☐ Are multiple contact channels available?
- ☐ Is there an FAQ that answers likely questions?
- ☐ Is it clear what response time to expect?

For Each Friction Point Identified: What is the friction? Why does it exist? Is it necessary (does it serve a purpose)? If not necessary: how can it be removed? If necessary: how can it be reduced or made more bearable?

Pilot Storytelling Framework

Use this framework to capture and deploy stories from pilots for broader rollout.

Before the Pilot (Baseline Documentation): Team/participant description. Starting situation (be specific about challenges). Metrics at baseline. Participant expectations and concerns (captured in their words).

During the Pilot (Ongoing Capture): Week-by-week observations. Turning points and breakthrough moments. Challenges encountered and how addressed. Quotes from participants (captured in the moment). Unexpected outcomes.

After the Pilot (Results Documentation): Metrics at completion (compared to baseline). Qualitative changes observed. Participant testimonials (structured).

Testimonial Questions: What were you most worried about before we started? What surprised you about the experience? What's specifically different about your work now? What would you tell a colleague who's sceptical? What would you go back and tell yourself at the beginning?

The Story (Structured for Deployment):

Before (30 seconds): Vivid description of the starting point. Specific challenges, frustrations, or limitations. Paint the picture of what life was like.

The transition (30 seconds): What changed? What was the experience of adopting the new approach? Acknowledge difficulty honestly.

The breakthrough (30 seconds): When did things click? What was the moment when the value became clear?

After (30 seconds): Where are things now? Specific improvements, quantified where possible. How do people feel?

The lesson (30 seconds): What does this mean for others? Why should they believe this could work for them?

Story Deployment Checklist

☐ Written summary for communications

☐ Participant willing to speak/be quoted

☐ Video testimonial captured (if appropriate)

☐ Before-and-after data visualised

☐ Story incorporated into rollout communications

☐ Advocates briefed and ready to support

Appendix B: Measurement Frameworks

Dual-Dashboard Setup Guide

Performance Dashboard (Weekly Review)

This dashboard tracks operational effectiveness. Is your communication machinery working?

Metric one: Reach. Definition: Percentage of target audience who received the communication. Calculation: (Number delivered / Target audience size) × 100. Target: Varies by channel; establish baseline then improve.

Metric two: Engagement. Definition: Percentage of recipients who engaged with the communication. Calculation: (Number who opened, clicked, or attended / Number delivered) × 100. Note: Distinguish between passive engagement (opens) and active engagement (clicks, attendance, responses). Target: Establish baseline by communication type; compare like with like.

Metric three: Action completion. Definition: Percentage who completed required action (where applicable). Calculation: (Number who completed action / Number delivered) × 100. Note: Only applicable for communications with specific calls to action. Target: Depends on action type; mandatory actions should approach 100%.

Metric four: Support volume. Definition: Number of questions or issues raised. Tracking: Log all questions by channel, topic, and date. Analysis: High volume may indicate unclear communication; categorise to identify patterns.

Metric five: Response time. Definition: Average time to acknowledge and resolve questions. Calculation: Track time from question received to acknowledgment and to resolution. Target: Per your service level agreement.

Brand Dashboard (Quarterly Review)

This dashboard tracks relationship health. Is your communication approach building or eroding trust?

Metric one: Trust pulse (composite score). Components: Average of core survey questions. Scale: Typically 1-5 or 1-7; convert to percentage for easier interpretation. Trend: Direction matters more than absolute number; track quarter over quarter.

Metric two: Comprehension. Definition: Percentage who can accurately describe key messages. Method: Survey sample with open-ended questions; evaluate responses for accuracy. Calculation: (Number of accurate responses / Number surveyed) × 100. Target: Establish baseline; aim for consistent improvement.

Metric three: Repeat engagement. Definition: Percentage who engage with multiple communications over time. Calculation: (Number engaging with 3+ of last 5 communications / Total audience) × 100. Trend: Indicates whether people find sustained value.

Metric four: Internal NPS. Definition: Net Promoter Score for communications. Question: "How likely are you to recommend how this organisation communicates to someone considering a job here?" Calculation: % Promoters (9-10) minus % Detractors (0-6). Range: -100 to +100; positive is good, above +30 is strong.

Metric five: Sentiment trend. Definition: Directional indicator of how feeling about communications is shifting. Method: Qualitative analysis of comments, questions, and feedback. Tracking: Categorise as positive, neutral, or negative; track proportions over time.

Sample Survey Questions

Trust Pulse Questions (Core Set): Use these questions consistently over time. Do not change wording; consistency enables comparison.

Trust: "I trust the information I receive from leadership."

Comprehension: "I understand the organisation's direction and priorities."

Relevance: "Communications from the organisation are relevant to my work."

Timeliness: "When something important happens, I hear about it through official channels before I hear about it through rumour."

Support: "When I have questions about organisational communications, I know where to get answers."

(All questions use: Strongly disagree / Disagree / Neutral / Agree / Strongly agree)

Comprehension Testing Questions: Use these to test actual understanding rather than satisfaction.

"In your own words, what are the organisation's top three priorities this year?" (Evaluate responses for accuracy against actual priorities)

"What is the main reason behind [specific recent change]?" (Evaluate responses for accuracy against intended message)

"As a result of [specific communication], what should you do differently?" (Evaluate responses for accuracy against intended action)

Benchmark Ranges

Use these ranges as general guidance. Your specific context matters more than industry benchmarks.

Performance Metrics

Email open rates: Below 30%: Concern. 30-50%: Typical range. Above 50%: Strong. Above 70%: Exceptional.

Town hall attendance: Below 40%: Concern. 40-60%: Typical range. Above 60%: Strong. Above 80%: Exceptional.

Action completion (mandatory): Below 70%: Concern. 70-85%: Typical range. 85-95%: Strong. Above 95%: Exceptional.

Question response time: Same day acknowledgment: Target for significant communications. Within 24 hours substantive response: Reasonable. Within 3 business days for complex questions: Acceptable. Longer than 3 days: Risk of trust erosion.

Brand Metrics

Trust pulse score (5-point scale): Below 3.0: Concern. 3.0-3.5: Below par. 3.5-4.0: Adequate. 4.0-4.5: Strong. Above 4.5: Exceptional.

Comprehension accuracy: Below 40%: Concern. 40-60%: Typical but inadequate. 60-80%: Adequate. Above 80%: Strong.

Repeat engagement: Below 30%: Concern. 30-50%: Typical. 50-70%: Strong. Above 70%: Exceptional.

Internal NPS: Below 0: Concern. 0-20: Below par. 20-40: Adequate. Above 40: Strong. Above 60: Exceptional.

Appendix C: Further Reading

Behavioural Economics and Psychology

Thinking, Fast and Slow by Daniel Kahneman. The foundational text on cognitive biases and how humans actually make decisions. Essential reading for understanding why people don't process information the way we expect them to.

Predictably Irrational by Dan Ariely. Accessible exploration of irrational behaviour patterns. Particularly useful chapters on the psychology of expectations, the power of free, and the influence of context on perception.

Nudge by Richard Thaler and Cass Sunstein. How small changes in how choices are presented can dramatically affect outcomes. Directly applicable to how communications are structured and framed.

The Psychology of Waiting Lines by David Maister. The original paper on why uncertain waits feel longer than certain ones. Short, practical, and directly relevant to managing communication during change.

Influence by Robert Cialdini. The classic text on persuasion psychology. The chapters on social proof, commitment, and scarcity are particularly relevant to internal communications.

Brand Theory and Marketing

The Long and the Short of It by Les Binet and Peter Field. The research behind the 60/40 brand-to-performance ratio discussed in Chapter Two. Essential reading for understanding why meaning-building and action-driving communications need different balances.

How Brands Grow by Byron Sharp. Challenges conventional marketing wisdom with evidence-based findings. The principles about mental availability and reach have implications for internal audience engagement.

Building a StoryBrand by Donald Miller. Practical framework for clarifying message through narrative structure. The approach translates well to internal communications.

Made to Stick by Chip Heath and Dan Heath. Why some ideas survive and others die. The SUCCESS framework (Simple, Unexpected, Concrete, Credible, Emotional, Stories) provides a useful checklist for memorable communications.

Experience Design

The Power of Moments by Chip Heath and Dan Heath. How to create defining experiences through elevation, insight, pride, and connection. Directly applicable to designing communication moments rather than just messages.

Hooked by Nir Eyal. The psychology of habit-forming products. The principles of trigger, action, variable reward, and investment apply to creating communications that people return to.

The Design of Everyday Things by Don Norman. Foundational text on user-centred design. The principles of visibility, feedback, and mapping apply directly to communication design.

Designing for Behavior Change by Stephen Wendel. Practical framework for using behavioural science in product design. The CREATE action funnel provides a useful model for communication effectiveness.

Organisational Communication

Simply Said by Jay Sullivan. Practical guide to clear business communication. Particularly useful for training others in your organisation on communication fundamentals.

The Culture Map by Erin Meyer. How cultural differences affect communication across global organisations. Essential reading for anyone communicating across borders or diverse teams.

Crucial Conversations by Kerry Patterson and colleagues. Framework for high-stakes communication. The principles apply to both interpersonal and organisational communication during difficult topics.

Switch by Chip Heath and Dan Heath. How to change when change is hard. The framework of directing the rider, motivating the elephant, and shaping the path provides a useful model for change communications.

Measurement and Analytics

Measuring the User Experience by Tom Tullis and Bill Albert. Practical guide to user research and measurement. The principles translate well to measuring communication effectiveness.

How to Measure Anything by Douglas Hubbard. Framework for quantifying things that seem impossible to measure. Useful for thinking about how to measure understanding and trust.

Lean Analytics by Alistair Croll and Benjamin Yoskovitz. How to use data to build better products. The principle of focusing on one metric that matters applies to communication measurement.

Storytelling

The Storytelling Animal by Jonathan Gottschall. Why humans are wired for narrative. Provides the scientific foundation for why stories work in communications.

Story by Robert McKee. The craft of narrative structure. Written for screenwriters but the principles of setup, conflict, and resolution apply to organisational storytelling.

Lead with a Story by Paul Smith. Collection of business stories with analysis of why they work. Useful source of examples and inspiration for organisational narratives.

Whoever Tells the Best Story Wins by Annette Simmons. Practical guide to using stories in business contexts. The framework of six stories you need to know how to tell is particularly applicable.

Change Management

Managing Transitions by William Bridges. The human side of organisational change. The distinction between change (situational) and transition (psychological) is essential for change communications.

Our Iceberg Is Melting by John Kotter. Fable illustrating the eight-step change model. Accessible introduction to change principles for sharing with non-specialists.

The Heart of Change by John Kotter and Dan Cohen. How successful change happens through emotion rather than analysis. The principle that people change when they feel differently, not just when they think differently, is central to effective change communications.

A Note on Sources

Many of the ideas in this book synthesise principles from multiple disciplines. The Target pregnancy prediction story in Chapter Eight was widely reported following Charles Duhigg's investigation for The New York Times in 2012. The "just add an egg" cake mix story has been told in various forms; the psychological insight is well-documented even if some historical details are debated. The Gmail scarcity strategy has been analysed in numerous business publications since Gmail's 2004 launch.

The London taxi Knowledge examination is documented by Transport for London and has been the subject of neuroscience research, including studies by Eleanor Maguire and colleagues at University College London examining how the intensive learning physically changes the brain.

The Significant Objects project by Rob Walker and Joshua Glenn is documented at significantobjects.com, where the original eBay listings and stories can still be reviewed.

The principles of behavioural economics referenced throughout draw heavily on the work of Daniel Kahneman, Amos Tversky, Richard Thaler, and their colleagues over several decades. The framing effect research discussed in Chapter Three was published by Tversky and Kahneman in Science in 1981.

Elizabeth Newton's tapping study, referenced in Chapter One as an illustration of the curse of knowledge, was her 1990 Stanford doctoral dissertation and was later popularised by Chip and Dan Heath in Made to Stick.

www.ingramcontent.com/pod-product-compliance
Lightning Source LLC
Chambersburg PA
CBHW031627210526
45464CB00004B/1786